ISBN 978-1-4400-8420-1
PIBN 10156808

This book is a reproduction of an important historical work. Forgotten Books uses
state-of-the-art technology to digitally reconstruct the work, preserving the original format
whilst repairing imperfections present in the aged copy. In rare cases, an imperfection in
the original, such as a blemish or missing page, may be replicated in our edition. We do,
however, repair the vast majority of imperfections successfully; any imperfections that
remain are intentionally left to preserve the state of such historical works.

For support please visit www.forgottenbooks.com

English
Français
Deutsche
Italiano
Español
Português

www.forgottenbooks.com

Mythology Photography **Fiction**
Fishing Christianity **Art** Cooking
Essays Buddhism Freemasonry
Medicine **Biology** Music **Ancient**
Egypt Evolution Carpentry Physics
Dance Geology **Mathematics** Fitness
Shakespeare **Folklore** Yoga Marketing
Confidence Immortality Biographies
Poetry **Psychology** Witchcraft
Electronics Chemistry History **Law**
Accounting **Philosophy** Anthropology
Alchemy Drama Quantum Mechanics
Atheism Sexual Health **Ancient History**
Entrepreneurship Languages Sport
Paleontology Needlework Islam
Metaphysics Investment Archaeology
Parenting Statistics Criminology
Motivational

AN ANNUAL OF
NEW POETRY

cv. l₂

1917

LONDON

CONSTABLE AND COMPANY LTD.

PR
1225
A584
197

PRINTED IN GREAT BRITAIN.
CHISWICK PRESS : CHARLES WHITTINGHAM AND CO.
TOOKS COURT, CHANCERY LANE, LONDON.

CONTENTS

v

Contents

Contents

GORDON BOTTOMLEY

Gordon Bottomley

THE PLOUGHMAN

UNDER the long fell's stony eaves
  The ploughman, going up and down,
Ridge after ridge man's tide-mark leaves,
And turns the hard grey soil to brown.

Striding, he measures out the earth
In lines of life, to rain and sun;
And every year that comes to birth
Sees him still striding on and on.

The seasons change, and then return;
 Yet still, in blind, unsparing ways,
However I may shrink or yearn,
 The ploughman measures out my days.

His acre brought forth roots last year;
This year it bears the gleamy grain;
Next Spring shall seedling grass appear:
Then roots and corn and grass again.

Five times the young corn's pallid green
I have seen spread and change and thrill;
Five times the reapers I have seen
Go creeping up the far-off hill:

And, as the unknowing ploughman climbs
Slowly and inveterately,
I wonder long how many times
The corn will spring again for me.

Gordon Bottomley

ATLANTIS

WHAT poets sang in Atlantis? Who can tell
The epics of Atlantis or their names?
The sea hath its own murmurs, and sounds not
The secrets of its silences beneath,
And knows not any cadences enfolded
When the last bubbles of Atlantis broke
Among the quieting of its heaving floor.

O, years and tides and leagues and all their billows
Can alter not man's knowledge of men's hearts—
While trees and rocks and clouds include our being
We know the epics of Atlantis still:
A hero gave himself to lesser men,
Who first misunderstood and murdered him,
And then misunderstood and worshipped him;
A woman was lovely and men fought for her,
Towns burnt for her, and men put men in bondage,
But she put lengthier bondage on them all;
A wanderer toiled among all the isles
That fleck this turning star of shifting sea,
Or lonely purgatories of the mind,
In longing for his home or his lost love.

Poetry is founded on the hearts of men:
Though in Nirvana or the Heavenly courts
The principle of beauty shall persist,
Its body of poetry, as the body of man,
Is but a terrene form, a terrene use,
That swifter being will not loiter with;
And, when mankind is dead and the world cold,
Poetry's immortality will pass.

Gordon Bottomley

A SURREY NIGHT

THROUGH bare black oak-boughs spread afar
I watch a sickle moon
Follow a large and lonely star
Beyond the low South Down.

The thin light films a wider sky
Than I have lived beneath;
The trees ebb out more distantly,
Past delicate wild heath.

But when the moonlight is so clear,
And the sharp night so still,
My thoughts will never settle here
Upon this gentle hill;

For when the moonlight is so pale
Above dark fields and woods,
I only see my Northern vale
And its steep solitudes;

The hard, lean fells against the night,
Between the darker trees;
The high and distant farm-house light;
The village stillnesses.

I hear the larch-wood brook draw near,
Lapper and lull and leap,
In far-off night, that I would hear
Before I go to sleep.

Gordon Bottomley

AVELINGLAS

NOW whether land or water win,
The sky will still be drear;
There's no place for King Avelin
Who built his palace here.

Between the river and the tide
Only one street may stand,
But once the streets were seven and wide
Before men came to the sand.

King Avelin steered out of the North,
In the time of the swans' flight;
And whence his dark ships issued forth
None knew but a fog-bank white.

"This lonely haven is deep and clear,
This land will hold my folk;
And I shall build my palace here,
Beyond the Hairfair's yoke."

His daughter had a golden gown
That left her young neck bare,
And in the tower beyond the town
She washed her golden hair:

Through the window-hole she bowed
And dropped it in the sky;
She dried it till that waving cloud
Could make men's hearts beat high.

Gordon Bottomley

She washed her hair, she combed her hair
By night as well as day;
She swung it on the midnight air
To meet the rising spray.

She combed, and wrought the waking spell
Of the oldest wind on the sea—
" For then," she said, " the sea's swell
Will bring a lover to me."

The sea grew, the sky sank;
Streets made the long waves fret;
The river ran without a bank;
The housewives' knees were wet.

Tower and town, pine-wood and willow
Melted as though by rain;
And once the trough of a piling billow
Was paved with a golden mane.

King Avelin, King Avelin
Won to no kingly bier:
Ah, where is now King Avelin
Who built his palace here?

Gordon Bottomley

HOMUNCULUS IN PENUMBRA

"WHEN I look down my limbs and moving
        breast
I know that on a day these will commence
To contradict my being that bids them be
And sets the harmony by which they live.
I love to cleanse them; they reply to me,
Exuding, sloughing, duteously renewing,
For cleansing is the nature of their growth;
Yet in that day they shall deny my will,
And turn to filth, refuse, and dirty water,
While a dispersing sentience that was I
Stands close thereby in trouble, in travail
With words those lips delay to utter in time,
In awe-full agony lest that flesh dissolve
Before I can get into it again.

" And when I see it buried I shall cry out:
If it is given to fire I shall have throes
Of suffering, of unbearable regret,
Longing, apprehension, that shall bind
Yet, yet a little while the loosening wreaths
Of sentience that are continent of me:
Then shame and dread shall be the heart of me
Because I have no body to hide my thoughts,
That are being scanned, as if by unseen eyes,
Perused and judged, ineluctably judged,
I shivering in that exposury
Until dissemination is complete."

Gordon Bottomley

THE PRIDE OF WESTMORELAND

I MET a man of ninety-three
  Who took my hand in his,
He took my hand and shook my hand
And gave my wife a kiss;
" You've married the pride of Westmoreland "
He said, and he looked his fill—
But a hearty man of ninety-three
May kiss whomever he will.

There's a deal of truth and wisdom too
In a man of ninety-three,
Yet I did not need an aged man
To find the maid for me;
When I married the pride of Westmoreland
Youth's wisdom did not floor me—
I took my pick in Kendal town
Like Harry the Eighth before me.

Gordon Bottomley

SONG

THE maids went down to dip in the pool
　　When the mirrored moon had cooled the **water·**
But they never told the farmer's daughter,
For they knew she would tell her mother, the fool,
That the girls were out
And awaking the water,
With never a clout
Though the night was cool.

SINAI

I AM the Moses: I the mouth of God.
God speaking by me, I must choose His mode.
I understand how water stratifies:
Smiting, I change the balance of its force.
I recognize one element is all things,
So of bland dew blend my primeval food,
By morn and eve fulfil form's power to change.
This is my chisel, stylus of the God—
My hammer this: my hammer is God's mind.
I rule a naughty people and ignorant
By the wise wilful power dictated in me.
They watched me mount the mist with steps like threats;
When the mist took me they were still as blindness,
Uneasy and strained because I might return.
When man conceives his nature, his relation
To water, air, proud beasts, and fruiting trees,
No law can hold him but the law he makes;
His heart's reluctant, restless, clear perception
Only is simple and hard, is not avoided.
This is my freedom; this I figure as God
To guide a folk who do not free themselves.
A layer of stone can take law's burden, too,
Show forth my way most definitely and coldly·
Here in height's silence like my loneliness
I strike the steel to unavoidable things.

Gordon Bottomley

TO ——

WITH A PLAY

WITHIN your Roman house,
Your white and calm abode,
Your Lares in their niche
(Nereid, nymph, and god)

Accept my alien vows
Of friendship to their friend;
By bronze and marble rich
You worship, yet I send

(I the old koroplast)
Image and figurine
Enamelled with gaudy plumes,
Corinthian, Pergamene.

Keep them until the last
Behind your Lares hidden:
Such mimes were meant for tombs,
Let them to yours be bidden.

Gordon Bottomley

NEW YEAR'S EVE, 1913

O, CARTMEL bells ring soft to-night,
And Cartmel bells ring clear,
But I lie far away to-night,
Listening with my dear;

Listening in a frosty land
Where all the bells are still
And the small-windowed bell-towers stand
Dark under heath and hill.

I thought that, with each dying year,
As long as life should last
The bells of Cartmel I should hear
Ring out an aged past:

The plunging, mingling sounds increase
Darkness's depth and height,
The hollow valley gains more peace
And ancientness to-night:

The loveliness, the fruitfulness,
The power of life lived there
Return, revive, more closely press
Upon that midnight air.

But many deaths have place in men
Before they come to die;
Joys must be used and spent, and then
Abandoned and passed by.

13

Gordon Bottomley

Earth is not ours; no cherished space
Can hold us from life's flow,
That bears us thither and thence by ways
We knew not we should go.

O, Cartmel bells ring loud, ring clear,
Through midnight deep and hoar,
A year new-born, and I shall hear
The Cartmel bells no more.

Gordon Bottomley

ALL SOULS, 1914

ON All Souls' night a year ago
The gentle, ghostly dead
Beat at my thoughts as moths beat low,
Near to my quiet bed,
Upon the pane; I did not know
What words they would have said.

They were remote within my mind,
Remote beyond the pane;
Whether with evil wills or kind,
They could not come again—
They had but swerved, as things resigned
To learn return was vain.

To-night the young uneasy dead
Obscure the moonless night;
Their energies of hope and dread,
Of passion and delight,
Are still unspent; their hearts unread
Surge mutinous in flight.

The life of earth beats in them yet,
Their pulses are not done;
They suffer by their nerves that fret
To feel no wind nor sun;
They fade, but cannot yet forget
Their conflicts are not won.

Gordon Bottomley

IN MEMORIAM

A. M. W.

Sᴇᴘᴛᴇᴍʙᴇʀ, 1910

(ꜰᴏʀ ᴀ ꜱᴏʟᴇᴍɴ ᴍᴜꜱɪᴄ)

OUT of a silence
The voice of music speaks.

When words have no more power,
When tears can tell no more,
The heart of all regret
Is uttered by a falling wave
Of melody.

No more, no more
The voice that gathered us
Shall hush us with deep joy;
But in this hush,
Out of its silence,
In the awaking of music,
It shall return.

For music can renew
Its gladness and communion,
Until we also sink,
Where sinks the voice of music,
Into a silence.

W. H. DAVIES

W H. Davies

BROTHERS

THEY lived together day and night,
　　Two brothers, all alone:
Six weeks had gone, and neighbours said—
　　"We see no more than one.

"Where is thy brother Charlie, Tom,
　　And is he sick?" they said.
Said Tom, that man so queer and quaint—
　　"My brother's still in bed."

And every night they heard his voice,
　　Down on the stairs below:
"And are you still in bed and sick—
　　How are you, Charlie, now?"

They forced the doors and entered in,
　　Found Charlie on the bed:
"I see a dead man here alive,"
　　The old physician said.

"For see the worms—they bubble here
　　In pools upon his flesh:
They wag the beard that's on his chin—
　　This body is not fresh."

Then came a voice all sharp and clear,
　　Down on the stairs below:
"And are you still in bed and sick—
　　How are you, Charlie, now?"

THE BELL

IT is the bell of death I hear,
   Which tells me my own time is near;
When I must join those quiet souls
Where nothing lives but worms and moles;
And not come through the grass again,
Like worms and moles, for breath or rain;
Yet let none weep when my life's through,
For I myself have wept for few.

The only things that knew me well
Were children, dogs, and girls that fell;
I bought poor children cakes and sweets,
Dogs heard my voice and danced the streets;
And, gentle to a fallen lass,
I made her weep for what she was.
Good men and women know not me,
Nor love nor hate the mystery.

W. H. Davies

IN ENGLAND

WE have no grass locked up in ice so fast
That cattle cut their faces and at last,
When it is reached, must lie them down and starve—
Their bleeding mouths being froze too hard to move.
We have not that delirious state of cold
That makes men warm and sing when in Death's hold.
We have no roaring floods whose angry shocks
Can kill the fishes dashed against their rocks.
We have no winds that cut down street by street,
As easy as our scythes can cut down wheat.
No mountains here to spew their burning hearts
Into the valleys, on our human parts.
No earthquakes here, that ring church bells afar,
A hundred miles from where those earthquakes are.
We have no cause to set our dreaming eyes,
Like Arabs, on fresh streams in Paradise.
We have no wilds to harbour men that tell
More murders than they can remember well.
No woman here shall wake from her night's rest,
And find a snake is sucking at her breast.
Though I have travelled many and many a mile,
And had a man to black my boots and smile
With teeth that had less bone in them than gold—
Give me this England now, for all my world.

JOVE WARNS US

JOVE warns us with his lightning first,
  Before he sends his thunder;
Before the cock begins to crow,
  He claps his wings down under.
But I, who go to see a maid,
  This springtime in the morning,
Fall under every spell she has,
  Without a word of warning.

She little thinks what charms her breath
  To cunning eyes reveal;
The waves that down her body glide,
  That from her bosom steal.
Her moth-like plumpness caught my eye,
  I watched it like a spider;
By her own hair my web is made,
  To fasten me beside her.

W. H. Davies

ANGEL AND MYSTERY

LO, I, that once was Fear, that hears
His own forgotten breath, and fears
The breath of something else is heard—
Am now bold Love, to dare the word;
No timid mouse am I, before
He'll cross a moonbeam on the floor.
So, sit thou close, and I will pour
Into that rosy shell, thy ear,
My deep-sea passion; let me swear
There's nothing in this world as fair
As thy sweet face that does, and will,
Retain its baby roundness still:
With those two suns, thine eyes, that keep
Their light from clouds till Night brings sleep.
Forget my features, only see
The soul in them that burns for thee;
And never let it cross thy mind
That I am ugly for my kind;
Although the world may well declare,
"One is an angel sweet and fair;
But what it is that sits so close,
Must rest with God—He only knows."

JOHN DRINKWATER

John Drinkwater

MY ESTATE

I HAVE four loves, four loves are mine,
    My wife who makes all beauty be,
Tom Squire and Master Candleshine,
    And then my grey dog Timothy.

My wife makes bramble-berry pies,
    And she is bright as bramble dew,
She knows the way the weather flies,
    And tells me every thing to do.

Tom Squire he is my neighbour man,
    His apples fall upon my grass,
And in the morning, when we can,
    We say good-morning as we pass.

And Master Candleshine the True,
    Considering some fault of mine,
Says—"Had it been for me to do,
    It had been hard for Candleshine."

When I have thought all things that be,
    And drop the latch and climb the stair,
And want an eye for company,
    My grey dog Timothy is there.

My loves are one and two and three
    And four they are, good loves of mine,
Tom Squire, my grey dog Timothy,
    My wife and Master Candleshine.

John Drinkwater

ON READING THE MS. OF DOROTHY WORDSWORTH'S JOURNALS

TO-DAY I read the poet's sister's book,
She who so comforted those Grasmere days
When song was at the flood, and thence I took
A larger note of fortitude and praise.

And in her ancient fastness beauty stirred,
And happy faith was in my heart again,
Because the virtue of a simple word
Was durable above the lives of men.

For reading there that quiet record made
Of skies and hills, domestic hours, and free
Traffic of friends, and song, and duty paid,
I touched the wings of immortality.

John Drinkwater

JUNE DANCE[1]

THE chestnut cones were in the lanes,
  Blushing, and eyed with ebony,
And young oak-apples lovingly
Clung to their stems with rosy veins
Threading their glossy amber; still
As wind may be, among the bloom
Of lilac and the burning broom
The dear wind moved deliciously,
And stayed upon the fragrant hill
And lightened on the sea;
And brushed the nettles nodding through
The budding globes of cloudy may,
And wavelike flowed upon the blue
Flowers of the woods.
              It was a day
When pearled blossom of peach and pear
Of blossoming season made an end,
Drifting along the sunlight, rare
Of beauty as thoughts between friend and friend
That have no cunning, but merely know
The way of truth for the heart is so.

It was such a time at the birth of June,
When the day was hushed at the hour of noon,
And whispering leaves gave out a tune
Ghostly as moves the bodiless moon
High in the full-day skies of June,

[1] Written 1908, re-written 1916.

That they passed, a throng
Of toilers whose eyes
Were dull with toiling, passed along
By a path that lies
Between the city of mean emprise
And a forest set in mellow lands,
Far out from the city of broken hands.

Meanly clad, with bodies worn,
They came upon the forest hour,
From open fields of springing corn
To cloistered shades
They passed, from June light to June bower,
Tall men, and maids
Deep-bosomed, apt for any seed
That life should passionately sow,
Yet pale and troubled of a creed
Cried out by men who nothing know
Of joy's diviner excellence.
Along the silent glades they stept,
Till, flowing in each drowsy sense,
June came upon them, and they slept.

Beneath cool clustered branch and bloom,
Littered with stars of amethyst,
Sun-arrows glancing through the gloom,
They slept; the lush young bracken kissed
The tired forms. Ah, wellaway,
Within so wide a peace to see
Fellows who measure every day
Merely the roads of misery.

Tall men, deep-bosomed maids were they,
As who should face the world and run

John Drinkwater

Fleet-footed down the laughing way,
With brows set fearless to the sun,
But slackened were the rippling thews
And all clean moods of courage dead,
Defeated by ignoble use
And sullen dread.

So in the sweet June-tide they slept,
Nor any dream of healing deep
Came over them; heart-sick they kept
A troubled sleep;
Companions of calamity,
Their sleep was but remembered pain,
And all their hunger but to be
Poor pilgrims in oblivion's train.

The stems each had a little shadow
In the early afternoon,
When the toilers first were lured
By a music long immured
In the central forest ways
Where no human footfall strays,
To the dreaming dance of June.

One by one they woke, their faces
Still with some new wonder,
As when in quiet shadowy places
Wandering hands may move asunder
Secret foliage, and intrude
On the ancestral solitude
Of some untutored forest thing—
Neither doubt nor fear they bring,
But just a strange new wonder.

John Drinkwater

So now the toilers woke. No thought
Of the old-time trouble came
Over them; the cares deep-wrought,
Furrowing, by years of shame,
Lightened, as upon their ears
Fell a music very low,
Sweet with moving of the years,
Burdened with the beat and flow
Of a garnered ecstasy
Gathered from the deeps of pain,
Music vaster than the sea,
Softer than the rain.

Then they rose,—the music played
But a little way ahead.
And with never question made
They were well to follow. Red
And gold and opal flashed the noon
On lichened trunk. Their raiment mean
Grew heavy in the dance of June,
And man and maid among the green
Unburdened them, and stood revealed
In clean unblushing loveliness,
Clear glowing limbs, all supple, steeled
And shining; many a streaming tress
Slipped beautiful to breast and knee,
They proved a world where was no sin,
Exultant, pure in passion, free,
Young captives bidden to begin
New being. Sweet the music called,
Promising immortal boon,
Swift they set their feet, enthralled,
To the dreaming dance of June.

John Drinkwater

They passed into the forest's heart,
Where the shadows thickened,
Soul and trembling body thrilled
With a joy new-quickened.
It was as though from early days
Their familiars
Had been the words of worship of the lonely woodland
      ways,
And the articulate voices of the stars.

      Keeping perfect measure
      To the music's chime,
      Reaping all the treasure
      Of the summer time,
      Noiselessly along the glades,
      Lithe white limbs all glancing,
      Comely men and comely maids
      Drifted in their dancing.

When chestnut cones were in the lanes,
Blushing, and eyed with ebony,
And young oak-apples lovingly
Clung to their stems with rosy veins
Threading their glossy amber—then
They took them to faring, maids and men,
Whose eyes were dull with toiling, far
From their toil in the time of a perfect noon,
To where the quiet shadows are,
And joined the dreaming dance of June.

EDWARD EASTAWAY

OLD MAN

OLD Man, or Lad's-love,—in the name there's
    nothing
To one that knows not Lad's-love, or Old Man,
The hoar-green feathery herb, almost a tree,
Growing with rosemary and lavender.
Even to one that knows it well, the names
Half decorate, half perplex, the thing it is:
At least, what that is clings not to the names
In spite of time. And yet I like the names.

The herb itself I like not, but for certain
I love it, as some day the child will love it
Who plucks a feather from the door-side bush
Whenever she goes in or out of the house.
Often she waits there, snipping the tips and shrivelling
The shreds at last on to the path, perhaps
Thinking, perhaps of nothing, till she sniffs
Her fingers and runs off. The bush is still
But half as tall as she, though it is as old;
So well she clips it. Not a word she says;
And I can only wonder how much hereafter
She will remember, with that bitter scent,
Of garden rows, and ancient damson-trees
Topping a hedge, a bent path to a door,
A low thick bush beside the door, and me
Forbidding her to pick.

              As for myself,
Where first I met the bitter scent is lost.

Edward Eastaway

I, too, often shrivel the grey shreds,
Sniff them and think and sniff again and try
Once more to think what it is I am remembering,
Always in vain. I cannot like the scent,
Yet I would rather give up others more sweet,
With no meaning, than this bitter one.

I have mislaid the key. I sniff the spray
And think of nothing; I see and I hear nothing;
Yet seem, too, to be listening, lying in wait
For what I should, yet never can, remember:
No garden appears, no path, no hoar-green bush
Of Lad's-love, or Old Man, no child beside,
Neither father nor mother, nor any playmate;
Only an avenue, dark, nameless, without end.

Edward Eastaway

SNOW

IN the gloom of whiteness,
   In the great silence of snow,
A child was sighing
And bitterly saying: "Oh,
They have killed a white bird up there on her nest,
The down is fluttering from her breast."
And still it fell through that dusky brightness
On the child crying for the bird of the snow.

Edward Eastaway

THE CUCKOO

THAT'S the cuckoo, you say. I cannot hear it.
   When last I heard it I cannot recall; but I know
Too well the year when first I failed to hear it—
It was drowned by my man groaning out to his sheep
      "Ho! Ho!"

Ten times with an angry voice he shouted
"Ho! Ho!" but not in anger, for that was his way.
He died that Summer, and that is how I remember
The cuckoo calling, the children listening, and me say-
      ing, "Nay"

And now, as you said, "There it is" I was hearing
Not the cuckoo at all, but my man's "Ho! Ho!" instead.
And I think that even if I could lose my deafness
The cuckoo's note would be drowned by the voice of my
      dead.

Edward Eastaway

THE NEW HOUSE

NOW first, as I shut the door,
　　I was alone
In the new house; and the wind
　　Began to moan.

Old at once was the house,
　　And I was old;
My ears were teased with the dread
　　Of what was foretold,

Nights of storm, days of mist, without end;
　　Sad days when the sun
Shone in vain: old griefs, and griefs
　　Not yet begun.

All was foretold me; naught
　　Could I foresee;
But I learnt how the wind would sound
　　After these things should be.

Edward Eastaway

WIND AND MIST

THEY met inside the gateway that gives the view,
  A hollow land as vast as heaven. "It is
A pleasant day, sir." "A very pleasant day."
"And what a view here. If you like angled fields
Of grass and grain bounded by oak and thorn,
Here is a league. Had we with Germany
To play upon this board it could not be
More dear than April has made it with a smile.
The fields beyond that league close in together
And merge, even as our days into the past,
Into one wood that has a shining pane
Of water. Then the hills of the horizon—
That is how I should make hills had I to show
One who would never see them what hills were like."
"Yes. Sixty miles of South Downs at one glance.
Sometimes a man feels proud at them, as if
He had just created them with one mighty thought."
"That house, though modern, could not be better
      planned
For its position. I never liked a new
House better. Could you tell me who lives in it?"
"No one." "Ah—and I was peopling all
Those windows on the south with happy eyes,
The terrace under them with happy feet;
Girls—" "Sir, I know. I know. I have seen that
      house
Through mist look lovely as a castle in Spain,

And airier. I have thought: ' 'Twere happy there
To live.' And I have laughed at that
Because I lived there then." "Extraordinary."
" Yes, with my furniture and family
Still in it, I, knowing every nook of it
And loving none, and in fact hating it."
" Dear me! How could that be? But pardon me."
" No offence. Doubtless the house was not to blame,
But the eye watching from those windows saw,
Many a day, day after day, mist—mist
Like chaos surging back—and felt itself
Alone in all the world, marooned alone.
We lived in clouds, on a cliff's edge almost
(You see), and if clouds went, the visible earth
Lay too far off beneath and like a cloud.
I did not know it was the earth I loved
Until I tried to live there in the clouds
And the earth turned to cloud." "You had a garden
Of flint and clay, too." "True; that was real enough.
The flint was the one crop that never failed.
The clay first broke my heart, and then my back ;
And the back heals not. There were other things
Real, too. In that room at the gable a child
Was born while the wind chilled a summer dawn:
Never looked grey mind on a greyer one
Than when the child's cry broke above the groans."
" I hope they were both spared." "They were. Oh yes.
But flint and clay and childbirth were too real
For this cloud castle. I had forgot the wind.
Pray do not let me get on to the wind.
You would not understand about the wind.
It is my subject, and compared with me
Those who have always lived on the firm ground
Are quite unreal in this matter of the wind.

Edward Eastaway

There were whole days and nights when the wind and I
Between us shared the world, and the wind ruled
And I obeyed it and forgot the mist.
My past and the past of the world were in the wind.
Now you will say that though you understand
And feel for me, and so on, you yourself
Would find it different. You are all like that
If once you stand here free from wind and mist:
I might as well be talking to wind and mist.
You would believe the house-agent's young man
Who gives no heed to anything I say.
Good morning. But one word. I want to admit
That I would try the house once more, if I could;
As I should like to try being young again."

Edward Eastaway

THE UNKNOWN

SHE is most fair,
   And when they see her pass
The poets' ladies
Look no more in the glass
But after her.

On a bleak moor
Running under the moon
She lures a poet,
Once proud or happy, soon
Far from his door.

Beside a train,
Because they saw her go,
Or failed to see her,
Travellers and watchers know
Another pain.

The simple lack
Of her is more to me
Than others' presence,
Whether life splendid be
Or utter black.

I have not seen,
I have no news of her;
I can tell only
She is not here, but there
She might have been.

She is to be kissed
Only perhaps by me;
She may be seeking
Me and no other: she
May not exist.

Edward Eastaway

THE WORD

THERE are so many things I have forgot,
That once were much to me, or that were not,
All lost, as is a childless woman's child
And its child's children, in the undefiled
Abyss of what can never be again.
I have forgot, too, names of the mighty men
That fought and lost or won in the old wars,
Of kings and fiends and gods, and most of the stars.
Some things I have forgot that I forget.
But lesser things there are, remembered yet,
Than all the others. One name that I have not—
Though 'tis an empty thingless name—forgot
Never can die because Spring after Spring
Some thrushes learn to say it as they sing.
There is always one at midday saying it clear
And tart—the name, only the name I hear.
While perhaps I am thinking of the elder scent
That is like food, or while I am content
With the wild rose scent that is like memory,
This name suddenly is cried out to me
From somewhere in the bushes by a bird
Over and over again, a pure thrush word.

Edward Eastaway

AFTER RAIN

THE rain of a night and a day and a night
    Stops at the light
Of this pale choked day. The peering sun
Sees what has been done.
The road under the trees has a border new
Of purple hue
Inside the border of bright thin grass:
For all that has
Been left by November of leaves is torn
From hazel and thorn
And the greater trees. Throughout the copse
No dead leaf drops
On grey grass, green moss, burnt-orange fern,
At the wind's return:
The leaflets out of the ash-tree shed
Are thinly spread
In the road, like little black fish, inlaid,
As if they played.
What hangs from the myriad branches down there
So hard and bare
Is twelve yellow apples lovely to see
On one crab-tree,
And on each twig of every tree in the dell
Uncountable
Crystals both dark and bright of the rain
That begins again.

Edward Eastaway

ASPENS

ALL day and night, save winter, every weather,
Above the inn, the smithy, and the shop,
The aspens at the cross-roads talk together
Of rain, until their last leaves fall from the top.

Out of the blacksmith's cavern comes the ringing
Of hammer, shoe, and anvil; out of the inn
The clink, the hum, the roar, the random singing—
The sounds that for these fifty years have been.

The whisper of the aspens is not drowned,
And over lightless pane and footless road,
Empty as sky, with every other sound
Not ceasing, calls their ghosts from their abode,

A silent smithy, a silent inn, nor fails
In the bare moonlight or the thick-furred gloom,
In tempest or the night of nightingales,
To turn the cross-roads to a ghostly room

And it would be the same were no house near.
Over all sorts of weather, men, and times,
Aspens must shake their leaves and men may hear
But need not listen, more than to my rhymes.

Whatever wind blows, while they and I have leaves
We cannot other than an aspen be
That ceaselessly, unreasonably grieves,
Or so men think who like a different tree.

A PRIVATE

THIS ploughman dead in battle slept out of doors
    Many a frosty night, and merrily
Answered staid drinkers, good bedmen, and all bores:
" At Mrs. Greenland's Hawthorn Bush," said he,
" I slept." None knew which bush. Above the town,
Beyond " The Drover," a hundred spot the down
In Wiltshire. And where now at last he sleeps
More sound in France—that, too, he secret keeps.

Edward Eastaway

SEDGE WARBLERS

THIS beauty made me dream there was a time
Long past and irrecoverable, a clime
Where any brook so radiant racing clear
Through buttercup and kingcup bright as brass
But gentle, nourishing the meadow grass
That leans and scurries in the wind, would bear
Another beauty, divine and feminine,
Child to the sun, a nymph whose soul unstained
Could love all day, and never hate or tire,
A lover of mortal or immortal kin.

And yet, rid of this dream, ere I had drained
Its poison, quieted was my desire
So that I only looked into the water,
Clearer than any goddess or man's daughter,
And hearkened while it combed the dark green hair
And shook the millions of the blossoms white
Of water-crowfoot, and curdled to one sheet
The flowers fallen from the chestnuts in the park
Far off. And sedge-warblers, clinging so light
To willow twigs, sang longer than the lark,
Quick, shrill, or grating, a song to match the heat
Of the strong sun, nor less the water's cool,
Gushing through narrows, swirling in the pool.
Their song that lacks all words, all melody,
All sweetness almost, was dearer then to me
Than sweetest voice that sings in tune sweet words.
This was the best of May—the small brown birds
Wisely reiterating endlessly
What no man learnt yet, in or out of school.

51

Edward Eastaway

FOR THESE

AN acre of land between the shore and the hills,
Upon a ledge that shows my kingdoms three,
The lovely visible earth and sky and sea,
Where what the curlew needs not, the farmer tills:

A house that shall love me as I love it,
Well-hedged, and honoured by a few ash-trees
That linnets, greenfinches, and goldfinches
Shall often visit and make love in and flit:

A garden I need never go beyond,
Broken but neat, whose sunflowers every one
Are fit to be the sign of the Rising Sun:
A spring, a brook's bend, or at least a pond:

For these I ask not, but, neither too late
Nor yet too early, for what men call content,
And also that something may be sent
To be contented with, I ask of fate.

ROADS

I LOVE roads:
  The goddesses that dwell
Far along invisible
Are my favourite gods.

Roads go on
While we forget, and are
Forgotten like a star
That shoots and is gone.

On this earth 'tis sure
We men have not made
Anything that doth fade
So soon, so long endure:

The hill road wet with rain
In the sun would not gleam
Like a winding stream
If we trod it not again.

They are lonely
While we sleep, lonelier
For lack of the traveller
Who is now a dream only.

From dawn's twilight
And all the clouds like sheep
On the mountains of sleep
They wind into the night.

Edward Eastaway

The next turn may reveal
Heaven: upon the crest
The close pine clump, at rest
And black, may Hell conceal.

Often footsore, never
Yet of the road I weary,
Though long and steep and dreary
As it winds on for ever.

Helen of the roads,
The mountain ways of Wales
And the Mabinogion tales,
Is one of the true gods,

Abiding in the trees,
The threes and fours so wise,
The larger companies,
That by the roadside be,

And beneath the rafter
Else uninhabited
Excepting by the dead;
And it is her laughter

At morn and night I hear
When the thrush cock sings
Bright irrelevant things,
And when the chanticleer

Calls back to their own night
Troops that make loneliness
With their light footsteps' press,
As Helen's own are light.

Edward Eastaway

Now all roads lead to France
And heavy is the tread
Of the living; but the dead
Returning lightly dance:

Whatever the road bring
To me or take from me,
They keep me company
With their pattering,

Crowding the solitude
Of the loops over the downs,
Hushing the roar of towns
And their brief multitude.

Edward Eastaway

THE SOURCE

ALL day the air triumphs with its **two** voices
Of wind and rain:
As loud as if in anger it rejoices,
Drowning the sound of earth
That gulps and gulps in choked endeavour vain
To swallow the rain.

Half the night, too, only the wild air speaks
With wind and rain,
Till forth the dumb source of the river breaks
And drowns the rain and wind,
Bellows like a giant bathing in mighty mirth
The triumph of earth.

Edward Eastaway

LOVERS

THE two men in the road were taken aback.
The lovers came out shading their eyes from the
     sun,
And never was white so white, or black so black,
As her cheeks and hair. "There are more things than
     one
A man might turn into a wood for, Jack,"
Said George; Jack whispered: "He has not got a gun.
It's a bit too much of a good thing, I say.
They are going the other road, look. And see her
     run."—
She ran—"What a thing it is, this picking may."

BEAUTY

WHAT does it mean? Tired, angry, and ill at ease,
No man, woman, or child alive could please
Me now. And yet I almost dare to laugh
Because I sit and frame an epitaph—
" Here lies all that no one loved of him
And that loved no one." Then in a trice that whim
Has wearied. But, though I am like a river
At fall of evening while it seems that never
Has the sun lighted it or warmed it, while
Cross breezes cut the surface to a file,
This heart, some fraction of me, happily
Floats through the window even now to a tree
Down in the misting, dim-lit, quiet vale,
Not like a pewit that returns to wail
For something it has lost, but like a dove
That slants unswerving to its home and love.
There I find my rest, and through the dusk air
Flies what yet lives in me. Beauty is there.

Edward Eastaway

THE BROOK

SEATED once by a brook, watching a child
   Chiefly that paddled, I was thus beguiled.
Mellow the blackbird sang and sharp the thrush
Not far off in the oak and hazel brush,
Unseen. There was a scent like honeycomb
From mugwort dull. And down upon the dome
Of the stone the cart-horse kicks against so oft
A butterfly alighted. From aloft
He took the heat of the sun, and from below.
On the hot stone he perched contented so,
As if never a cart would pass again
That way; as if I were the last of men
And he the first of insects to have earth
And sun together and to know their worth.
I was divided between him and the gleam,
The motion, and the voices, of the stream,
The waters running frizzled over gravel,
That never vanish and for ever travel.
A grey flycatcher silent on a fence
And I sat as if we had been there since
The horseman and the horse lying beneath
The fir-tree-covered barrow on the heath,
The horseman and the horse with silver shoes,
Galloped the downs last. All that I could lose
I lost. And then the child's voice raised the dead.
"No one's been here before" was what she said
And what I felt, yet never should have found
A word for, while I gathered sight and sound.

SONG

AT poet's tears,
    Sweeter than any smiles but hers,
She laughs; I sigh;
And yet I could not live if she should die.

And when in June
Once more the cuckoo spoils his tune,
She laughs at sighs;
And yet she says she loves me till she dies.

ROBERT FROST

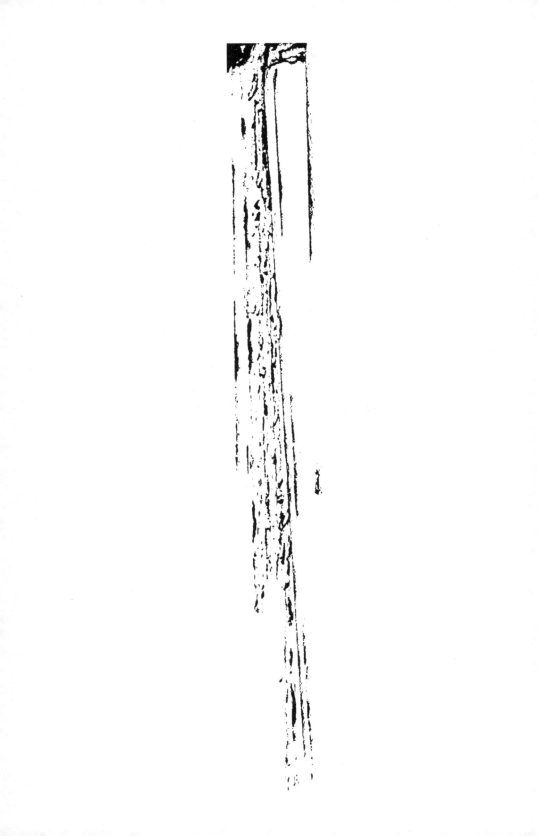

Robert Frost

CHRISTMAS TREES

(A CHRISTMAS CIRCULAR LETTER)

THE city had withdrawn into itself
  And left at last the country to the country;
When between whirls of snow not come to lie
And whirls of foliage not yet laid, there drove
A stranger to our yard, who looked the city,
Yet did in country fashion in that there
He sat and waited till he drew us out
A-buttoning coats to ask him who he was.
He proved to be the city come again
To look for something it had left behind
And could not do without and keep its Christmas.
He asked if I would sell my Christmas trees.
My woods—the young fir-balsams like a place
Where houses all are churches and have spires.
I hadn't thought of them as Christmas trees.
I doubt if I was tempted for a moment
To sell them off their feet to go in cars
And leave the slope behind the house all bare,
Where the sun shines now no warmer than the moon.
I'd hate to have them know it if I was.
Yet more I'd hate to hold my trees except
As others hold theirs or refuse for them,
Beyond the time of profitable growth,
The trial by market everything must come to.
I dallied so much with the thought of selling.
Then, whether from mistaken courtesy

And fear of seeming short of speech, or whether
From hope of hearing good of what was mine,
I said, "There aren't enough to be worth while."

"I could soon tell how many they would cut,
You let me look them over."
                                "You could look.
But don't expect I'm going to let you have them."

Pasture they spring in, some in clumps too close
That lop each other of boughs, but not a few
Quite solitary and having equal boughs
All round and round. The latter he nodded "Yes" to,
Or paused to say beneath some lovelier one
With buyer's moderation, "That would do."
I thought so too, but wasn't there to say so.

We climbed the pasture on the south, crossed over,
And came down on the north.
                              He said, "A thousand."

"A thousand Christmas trees!—at what a-piece?"

He felt some need of softening that to me:
"A thousand trees would come to thirty dollars."

Then I was certain I had never meant
To let him have them. Never show surprise!
But thirty dollars seemed so small beside
The extent of pasture I should strip, three cents
(For that was all they figured out a-piece)
Three cents so small beside the dollar friends
I should be writing to within the hour
Would pay in cities for good trees like those,

Robert Frost

Regular vestry-trees whole Sunday Schools
Could hang enough on to pick off enough.

A thousand Christmas trees I didn't know I had!
Worth three cents more to give away than sell,
As may be shown by a simple calculation.
Too bad I couldn't lay one in a letter.
I can't help wishing I could send you one,
In wishing you herewith a Merry Christmas.

Robert Frost

A GIRL'S GARDEN

A NEIGHBOR of mine in the village
Likes to tell how one spring
When she was a girl on the farm, she did
A childlike thing.

One day she asked her father
To give her a garden plot
To plant and tend and reap herself
And he said, " Why not? "

In casting about for a corner
He thought of an idle bit
Of walled-off ground where a shop had stood
And he said, " Just it! "

And he said, " That ought to make you
An *eye*deal one-girl farm,
And give you a chance to put some strength
On your slim-jim arm."

It was not enough of a garden,
Her father said, to plow.
So she had to work it all by hand,
But who cares now?

She wheeled the dung in a wheelbarrow
Along a stretch of road,
(But she always ran away and left
Her not-nice load

At the sound of anyone coming.)
And then she begged the seed.
She says she thinks she planted one
Of all things but weed:

A hill each of potatoes,
Radishes, lettuce, peas,
Tomatoes, pumpkins, beets, beans, corn,
And even fruit trees.

And yes, she has long mistrusted
That a cider apple tree
In bearing there to-day is hers,
Or at least may be.

Her crop was a miscellany
When all was said and done,
A little bit of everything,
A great deal of none.

Now when she sees in the village
How village things go,
Just when it seems to come in right
She says, " *I* know—

" It 's as when I was a farmer— "
Never by way of advice!
And she never sins by telling the tale
To the same person twice.

Robert Frost

THE LINE GANG

HERE come the line gang pioneering by.
　　They throw a forest down less cut than broken.
They plant dead trees for living, and the dead
They string together with a living thread.
They string an instrument against the sky
Wherein words, whether beaten out or spoken
Will run as hushed as when they were a thought.
But in no hush they string it: they go past
With shouts afar to pull the cable taut,
To hold it hard until they make it fast,
To ease away—they have it. With a laugh
An oath of towns that set the wild at naught,
They bring the telephone and telegraph.

Robert Frost

PEA BRUSH

I WALKED down alone Sunday after church
To the place where John has been cutting trees
To see for myself about the birch
He said I could have to bush my peas.

The sun in the new cut narrow gap
Was hot enough for the first of May,
And stifling hot with the odor of sap
From stumps still bleeding the life away.

The frogs that were peeping a thousand shrill
Wherever the ground was low and wet,
The minute they heard my step went still
To watch me and see what I came to get.

Birch boughs enough piled everywhere!—
All fresh and sound from the recent ax.
Time someone came with a cart and pair
And got them off the wild flowers' backs.

They might be good for garden things
To curl a little finger round,
The same as you seize cats-cradle strings,
And lift themselves up off the ground.

Small good to anything growing wild,
They were crooking many a trillium
That had budded before the boughs were piled,
And since it was coming up, had to come.

Robert Frost

THE OVEN BIRD

THERE is a singer everyone has heard,
Loud, a mid-summer and a mid-wood bird,
Who makes the solid tree-trunks sound again.
He says that leaves are old and that for flowers
Mid-summer is to spring as one to ten.
He says the early petal-fall is past
When pear and cherry bloom went down in showers
On sunny days a moment over-cast;
And comes that other fall we name the fal
He says the highway dust is over all.
The bird would cease and be as other birds
But that he knows in singing not to sing.
The question that he frames in all but words
Is what to make of a diminished thing.

Robert Frost

HYLA BROOK

BY June our brook's run out of song and speed.
  Sought for much after that it will be found
Either to have gone groping under ground
(And taken with it all the Hyla breed
That shouted in the mist a month ago
Like ghost of sleigh bells in the ghost of snow)
Or flourished and come up in jewel-weed,
Weak foliage that is blown upon and bent
Even against the way its waters went.
Its bed is left a faded paper sheet
Of dead leaves stuck together by the heat—
A brook to none but who remember long.
This as it will be seen is other far
Than with brooks taken otherwhere in song.
We love the things we love for what they are.

WILFRID WILSON GIBSON

Wilfrid Wilson Gibson

DAFFODILS

HE liked the daffodils. He liked to see
   Them nodding in the hedgerows cheerily
Along the dusty lanes as he went by—
Nodding and laughing to a fellow—Ay,
Nodding and laughing till you'ld almost think
They, too, enjoyed the jest.
                               Without a wink
That solemn butler said it, calm and smug,
Deep-voiced as though he talked into a jug:
" His lordship says he won't require no more
Crocks rivetted or mended till the war
Is over."
           Lord! He'd asked to have a wire
The moment that his lordship should desire
To celebrate the occasion fittingly
By a wild burst of mending crockery
Like a true Englishman, and hang expense!
He'd had to ask it, though he'd too much sense
To lift a lash or breathe a word before
His lordship's lordship closed the heavy door.
And then he'd laughed. Lord! but it did him good,
That quiet laugh. And somewhere in the wood
Behind the Hall there, a woodpecker laughed
Right out aloud as though he'd gone clean daft—
Right out aloud he laughed, the brazen bird,
As if he didn't care a straw who heard—

But then he'd not his daily bread to earn
By mending crocks.
                    And now at every turn
The daffodils were laughing quietly,
Nodding and laughing to themselves, as he
Chuckled : Now there's a patriot, real true-blue!

It seemed the daffodils enjoyed it too—
The fun of it. He wished that he could see—
Old solemn-mug—them laughing quietly
At him. But then, he'ld never have a dim
Idea they laughed, and, least of all, at him.
He'ld never dream they could be laughing at
A butler.
            'Twould be good to see the fat
Old peach-cheek in his solemn black and starch
Parading in his pompous parlour-march
Across that field of laughing daffodils.
'Twould be a sight to make you skip up hills,
Ay, crutch and all, and never feel your pack,
To see a butler in his starch and black
Among the daffodils, ridiculous
As that old bubbly-jock with strut and fuss—
Though that was rather rough upon the bird!
For all his pride, he didn't look absurd
Among the flowers—nor even that black sow
Grunting and grubbing in among them now.

And he was glad he hadn't got a trade
That starched the mother-wit in you, and made
A man look silly in a field of flowers.
'Twas better mending crocks, although for hours
You hobbled on—ay! and, maybe for days—
Hungry and cold along the muddy ways

Wilfrid Wilson Gibson

Without a job. And even when the sun
Was shining, 'twas not altogether fun
To lose the chance of earning a few pence
In these days: though 'twas well he'd got the sense
To see the funny side of things. It cost
You nothing, laughing to yourself. You lost
Far more by going fiddle-faced through life
Looking for trouble.

              He would tell his wife
When he got home. But lord, she'ld never see
What tickled him so mightily, not she!
She'ld only look up puzzled-like, and say
She didn't wonder at his lordship. Nay,
With tripe and trotters at the price they were
You'd got to count your coppers and take care
Of every farthing.

             Jack would see the fun—
Ay, Jack would see the joke. Jack was his son—
The youngest of the lot. And, man-alive,
'Twas queer that only one of all the five
Had got a twinkle in him—all the rest
Dull as ditchwater to the merriest jest.
Good lads enough they were, their mother's sons;
And they'd all pluck enough to face the guns
Out at the front. They'd got their mother's pluck:
And he was proud of them, and wished them luck.

That was no laughing matter—though 'twas well,
Maybe, if you could crack a joke in hell,
And shame the devil. Jack, at least, would fight
As well as any though his heart was light.
Jack was the boy for fighting and for fun;
And he was glad to think he'd got a son

Wilfrid Wilson Gibson

Who, even facing bloody death, would see
That little joke about the crockery,
And chuckle, as he charged.
                              His thoughts dropped back
Through eighteen years; and he again saw Jack
At the old home beneath the Malvern hills,
A little fellow plucking daffodils,
A little fellow who could scarcely walk,
Yet chuckling as he snapped each juicy stalk
And held up every yellow bloom to smell,
Poking his tiny nose into the bell
And sniffing its fresh scent, and chuckling still
As though he'd secrets with each daffodil.
Ay, he could see again the little fellow
In his blue frock among that laughing yellow,
And plovers in their sheeny black and white
Flirting and tumbling in the morning light
About his curly head. He still could see,
Shutting his eyes, as plain as plain could be,
Drift upon drift, those long-dead daffodils
Against the far green of the Malvern hills,
Nodding and laughing round his little lad,
As if to see him happy made them glad—
Nodding and laughing
                      They were nodding now,
The daffodils, and laughing—yet, somehow,
They didn't seem so merry now . . .
                              And he
Was fighting in a bloody trench maybe
For very life this minute
                          They missed Jack,
And he would give them all to have him back.

78

Wilfrid Wilson Gibson

THE PLOUGH

HE sniffed the clean and eager smell
Of crushed wild garlic, as he thrust
Beneath the sallows: and a spell
He stood there munching a thick crust—
The fresh tang giving keener zest
To bread and cheese—and watched a pair
Of wagtails preening wing and breast,
Then running—flirting tails in air,
And pied plumes sleeked to silky sheen—
Chasing each other in and out
The wet wild garlic's white and green.

And then remembering, with a shout,
And rattle whirring, he ran back
Again into the Fair Maid's Mead,
To scare the rascal thieves and black
That flocked from far and near to feed
Upon the sprouting grain. As one
They rose with clapping rustling wings—
Rooks, starlings, pigeons, in the sun
Circling about him in wide rings,
And plovers hovering over him
In mazy, interweaving flight—
Until it made his young wits swim
To see them up against the light,
A dazzling maze of black and white
Against the clear blue April sky—
Wings on wings in flashing flight
Swooping low and soaring high—

Wilfrid Wilson Gibson

Swooping, soaring, fluttering, flapping,
Tossing, tumbling, swerving, dipping,
Chattering, cawing, creaking, clapping,
Till he felt his senses slipping—
And gripped his corncrake rattle tight,
And flourished it above his head
Till every bird was out of sight:
And laughed, when all had flown and fled,
To think that he, and all alone,
Could put so many thieves to rout.

Then sitting down upon a stone
He wondered if the school were out—
The school where, only yesterday,
He'd sat at work among his mates—
At work that now seemed children's play,
With pens and pencils, books and slates—
Although he'd liked it well enough,
The hum and scuffling of the school,
And hadn't cared when Grim-and-Gruff
Would call him dunderhead and fool.

And he could see them sitting there—
His class-mates, in the lime-washed room,
With fingers inked and towzled hair—
Bill Baxter with red cheeks abloom,
And bright black eyes; and Ginger Jim
With freckled face and solemn look,
Who'd wink a pale blue eye at him,
Then sit intent upon his book,
While, caught a-giggle, he was caned.

He'd liked that room, he'd liked it all—
The window steaming when it rained;

Wilfrid Wilson Gibson

The sunlight dancing on the wall
Among the glossy charts and maps;
The blotchy stain beside the clock
That only he of all the chaps
Knew for a chart of Dead Man's Rock
That lies in Tiger Island Bay—
The reef on which the schooners split
And founder, that would bear away
The treasure-chest of Cut-throat-Kit,
That's buried under Black Bill's bones
Beneath the purple pepper-tree .
A trail of clean-sucked cherry-stones,
Which you must follow carefully,
Across the dunes of yellow sand
Leads winding upward from the beach
Till, with a pistol in each hand,
And cutlass 'twixt your teeth, you reach

Plumping their fat crops peacefully
Were plovers, pigeons, starlings, rooks,
Feeding on every side while he
Was in the land of story-books.
He raised his rattle with a shout
And scattered them with yell and crake
A man must mind what he's about
And keep his silly wits awake,
Not go wool-gathering, if he'ld earn
His wage. And soon, no schoolboy now,
He'ld take on a man's job, and learn
To build a rick, and drive the plough,
Like father . . .
                    Up against the sky
Beyond the spinney and the stream,
With easy stride and steady eye

Wilfrid Wilson Gibson

He saw his father drive his team,
Turning the red marl gleaming wet
Into long furrows clean and true.
And dreaming there, he longed to set
His young hand to the ploughshare too.

Wilfrid Wilson Gibson

THE DROVE ROAD

'TWAS going to snow—'twas snowing! Curse his
    luck!
And fifteen mile to travel—here was he
With nothing but an empty pipe to suck,
And half a flask of rum—but that would be
More welcome later on. He'd had a drink
Before he left; and that would keep him warm
A tidy while: and 'twould be good to think
He'd something to fall back on, if the storm
Should come to much. You never knew with snow.
A sup of rain he didn't mind at all,
But snow was different with so far to go—
Full fifteen mile, and not a house of call.
Ay, snow was quite another story, quite—
Snow on these fell-tops with a north-east wind
Behind it, blowing steadily with a bite
That made you feel that you were stark and skinned.

And those poor beasts —and they just off the boat
A day or so, and hardly used to land—
Still dizzy with the sea, their wits afloat.
When they first reached the dock, they scarce could stand,
They'd been so joggled. It's gey bad to cross,
After a long day's jolting in the train,
Thon Irish Channel, always pitch and toss—
And heads or tails, not much for them to gain!
And then the market, and the throng and noise

Wilfrid Wilson Gibson

Of yapping dogs: and they stung mad with fear,
Welted with switches by those senseless boys—
He'ld like to dust their jackets! But 'twas queer,
A beast's life, when you came to think of it
From start to finish—queerer, ay, a lot
Then any man's, and chancier a good bit.
With his ash-sapling at their heels they'd got
To travel before night those fifteen miles
Of hard fell-road, against the driving snow,
Half-blinded, on and on. He thought at whiles
'Twas just as well for them they couldn't know

Though, as for that, 'twas little that he knew
Himself what was in store for him. He took
Things as they came. 'Twas all a man could do;
And he'd kept going, somehow, by hook or crook.
And here was he, with fifteen mile of fell,
And snow, and .. God, but it was blowing stiff !
And no tobacco. Blest if he could tell
Where he had lost it—but, for half a whiff
He'ld swop the very jacket off his back—
Not that he'ld miss the cobweb of old shreds
That held the holes together.
           Thon Cheap-Jack
Who'd sold it him, had said it was Lord Ted's,
And London cut. But Teddy had grown fat
Since he'd been made an alderman   His bid?
And did the gentleman not want a hat
To go with it, a topper? If he did,
Here was the very . . .
           Hell, but it was cold:
And driving dark it was—nigh dark as night.
He'ld almost think he must be getting old,
To feel the wind so. And long out of sight

Wilfrid Wilson Gibson

The beasts had trotted. Well, what odds! The way
Ran straight for ten miles on, and they'ld go straight.
They'ld never heed a by-road. Many a day
He'd had to trudge on, trusting them to fate,
And always found them safe. They scamper fast,
But in the end a man could walk them down.
They're showy trotters; but they cannot last.
He'ld race the fastest beast for half-a-crown
On a day's journey. Beasts were never made
For steady travelling: drive them twenty mile,
And they were done; while he was not afraid
To tackle twice that distance with a smile.

But not a day like this! He'd never felt
A wind with such an edge. 'Twas like the blade
Of the rasper in the pocket of his belt
He kept for easy shaving. In his trade
You'd oft to make your toilet under a dyke—
And he was always one for a clean chin,
And carried soap.

        He'd never felt the like—
That wind, it cut clean through him to the skin.
He might be mother-naked, walking bare,
For all the use his clothes were, with the snow
Half-blinding him, and clagging to his hair,
And trickling down his spine. He'ld like to know
What was the sense of pegging steadily,
Chilled to the marrow, after a daft herd
Of draggled beasts he couldn't even see!

But that was him all over! Just a word,
A nod, a wink, the price of half-and-half—
And he'ld be setting out for God-knows-where,

Wilfrid Wilson Gibson

With no more notion than a yearling calf
Where he would find himself when he got there.
And he'd been travelling hard on sixty year
The same old road, the same old giddy gait;
And he'ld be walking, for a pint of beer,
Into his coffin, one day, soon or late—
But not with such a tempest in his teeth,
Half-blinded and half-dothered, that he hoped!
He'd met a sight of weather on the heath,
But this beat all.
          'Twas worse than when he'd groped
His way that evening down the Mallerstang—
Thon was a blizzard, thon—and he was done,
And almost dropping when he came a bang
Against a house—slap-bang, and like to stun—
Though that just saved his senses—and right there
He saw a lighted window he'd not seen,
Although he'd nearly staggered through its glare
Into a goodwife's kitchen, where she'd been
Baking hot girdle-cakes upon the peat.
And he could taste them now, and feel the glow
Of steady, aching, tingly, drowsy heat,
As he sat there and let the caking snow
Melt off his boots, staining the sanded floor.
And that brown jug she took down from the shelf—
And every time he'd finished, fetching more,
And piping: "Now reach up, and help yourself!"
She was a wonder, thon, the gay old wife—
But no such luck this journey. Things like that
Could hardly happen every day of life,
Or no one would be dying, but the fat
And oily undertakers, starved to death
For want of custom . . . Hell! but he would soon
Be giving them a job . . . It caught your breath,

That throttling wind. And it was not yet noon;
And he'ld be travelling through it until dark.
Dark? 'Twas already dark, and might be night
For all that he could see . . .

               And not a spark
Of comfort for him! Just to strike a light,
And press the kindling shag down in the bowl,
Keeping the flame well-shielded by his hand,
And puff, and puff! He'ld give his very soul
For half-a-pipe. He couldn't understand
How he had come to lose it. He'd the rum—
Ay, that was safe enough: but it would keep
Awhile, you never knew what chance might come
In such a storm . . .

            If he could only sleep . . .
If he could only sleep . . . That rustling sound
Of drifting snow, it made him sleepy-like—
Drowsy and dizzy, dithering round and round . .
If he could only curl up under a dyke,
And sleep and sleep .   It dazzled him, that white,
Drifting and drifting, round and round and round . .
Just half-a-moment's snooze . . . He'ld be all right.
It made his head quite dizzy, that dry sound
Of rustling snow. It made his head go round—
That rustling in his ears . . . and drifting, drifting
If he could only sleep .   he would sleep sound . .
God, he was nearly gone!

              The storm was lifting;
And he'd run into something soft and warm—
Slap into his own beasts, and never knew.
Huddled they were, bamboozled by the storm—
And little wonder either, when it blew
A blasted blizzard. Still, they'd got to go.
They couldn't stand there snoozing until night.

But they were sniffing something in the snow.
'Twas that had stopped them, something big and white—
A bundle—nay, a woman . . . and she slept.
But it was death to sleep.

                He'd nearly dropt
Asleep himself. 'Twas well that he had kept
That rum; and lucky that the beasts had stopt.

Ay, it was well that he had kept the rum.
He liked his drink: but he had never cared
For soaking by himself, and sitting mum.
Even the best rum tasted better, shared.

IN THE MEADOW

THE smell of wet hay in the heat
 All morning steaming round him rose,
As, in a kind of nodding doze,
Perched on the hard and jolting seat,
He drove the rattling, jangling rake
Round and around the Five Oaks Mead.
With that old mare he scarcely need
To drive at all or keep awake.
Gazing with half-shut, sleepy eyes
At her white flanks and grizzled tail
That flicked and flicked without avail
To drive away the cloud of flies
That hovered, closing and unclosing,
A shimmering hum and humming shimmer,
Dwindling dim and ever dimmer
In his dazzled sight, till, dozing,
He seemed to hear a murmuring stream
And gaze into a rippling pool
Beneath thick branches dark and cool—
And gazing, gazing till a gleam
Within the darkness caught his eyes,
He saw there smiling up at him
A young girl's face, now rippling dim,
Now flashing clear
                        Without surprise
He marked the eyes translucent blue,
The full red lips that seemed to speak,
The curves of rounded chin and cheek,

Wilfrid Wilson Gibson

The low, broad brow, sun-tanned . . .
He knew

That face, yet could not call to mind
Where he had seen it; and in vain
Strove to recall   .when sudden rain
Crashed down and made the clear pool blind,
And it was lost . . .
And, with a jerk
That well-nigh shook him from his seat,
He wakened to the steamy heat
And clank and rattle.
Still at work
The stolid mare kept on; and still
Over her hot, white flanks the flies
Hung humming. And his dazzled eyes
Closed gradually again, until
He dozed
And stood within the door
Of Dinchill dairy, drinking there
Thirst-quenching draughts of stone-cold air—
The scoured white shelves and sanded floor
And shallow milk-pans creamy white
Gleamed coldly in the dusky light .
And then he saw her, stooping down
Over a milk-pan, while her eyes
Looked up at him without surprise
Over the shoulder of her gown—
Her fresh print gown of speedwell blue
The eyes that looked out of the cool
Untroubled crystal of the pool
Looked into his again.
He knew
Those eyes now
From his dreamy doze

A sudden jolting of the rake
Aroused him.
                Startled, broad awake
He sat upright, lost in amaze
That he should dream of her—that lass!—
And see her face within the pool!

He'd known her always. Why, at school
They'd sat together in the class.
He'd always liked her well enough,
Young Polly Dale—and they had played
At Prisoners' Base and Who's Afraid,
At Tiggy and at Blindman's Buff,
A hundred times together . . .
                      Ay,
He'd always known her . . . It was strange,
Though he had noticed that a change
Had come upon her—she was shy,
And quieter, since she left school
And put her hair up—he'd not seen
Her face, till from the glancing sheen
It looked up at him from the pool

He'd always known her. Every day,
He'd nod to her as they would pass.
He'd always known her as a lass .
He'ld never know her just that way
Again now . . .
              In a different wise
They'ld meet—for how could he forget
His dream . . . The next time that they met
He'ld look into a woman's eyes.

Wilfrid Wilson Gibson

THE PLATELAYER

TAPPING the rails as he went by
  And driving the slack wedges tight,
He walked towards the morning sky
Between two golden lines of light
That dwindled slowly into one
Sheer golden rail that ran right on
Over the fells into the sun.

And dazzling in his eyes it shone,
That golden track, as left and right
He swung his clinking hammer—ay,
'Twas dazzling after that long night
In Hindfell tunnel, working by
A smoky flare, and making good
The track the rains had torn . . .
                          Clink, clink,
On the sound metal—on the wood
A duller thwack!
                  It made him blink,
That running gold . . .
                        'Twas sixteen hours
Since he'd left home—his garden smelt
So fragrant with the heavy showers
When he left home—and now he felt
That it would smell more fresh and sweet
After the tunnel's reek and fume
Of damp warm cinders. 'Twas a treat
To come upon the scent and bloom

That topped the cutting by the wood
After the cinders of the track,
The cinders and tarred sleepers—good
To lift your eyes from gritty black
Upon that blaze of green and red . . .
And she'ld be waiting by the fence,
And with the baby . . .
                  Straight for bed
He'ld make, if he had any sense,
And sleep the day; but, like as not,
When he'd had breakfast, he'ld turn to
And hoe the back potato-plot
'Twould be one mass of weeds he knew.
You'ld think each single drop of rain
Turned, as it fell, into a weed.
You seemed to hoe and hoe in vain.
Chickweed and groundsel didn't heed
The likes of him—and bindweed, well,
You hoed and hoed—still its white roots
Ran deeper
             'Twould be good to smell
The fresh-turned earth, and feel his boots
Sink deep into the brown wet mould,
After hard cinders . . .
              And, maybe,
The baby, sleeping good as gold
In its new carriage under a tree,
Would keep him company, while his wife
Washed up the breakfast-things.
                  'Twas strange,
The difference that she made to life,
That tiny baby-girl.
              The change
Of work would make him sleep more sound.

Wilfrid Wilson Gibson

'Twas sleep he needed. That long night
Shovelling wet cinders underground,
With breaking back—the smoky light
Stinging his eyes till they were sore . . .

He'd worked the night that she was born,
Standing from noon the day before
All through that winter's night till morn
Laying fog-signals on the line
Where it ran over Devil's Ghyll . . .

And she was born at half-past nine,
Just as he stood aside until
The Scots' Express ran safely by
He'd but to shut his eyes to see
Those windows flashing blindingly
A moment through the blizzard—he
Could feel again that slashing snow
That seemed to cut his face.
                                        But they,
The passengers, they couldn't know
What it cost him to keep the way
Open for them. So snug and warm
They slept or chattered, while he stood
And faced all night that raking storm—
The little house beside the wood
For ever in his thoughts: and he,
Not knowing what was happening . . .

But all went well as well could be
With Sally and the little thing.
And it had been worth while to wait
Through that long night with work to do,
To meet his mother at the gate

With such good news, and find it true,
Ay, truer than the truth.
                              He still
Could see his wife's eyes as he bent
Over the bairn . . .
                        The Devil's Ghyll
Had done its worst, and he was spent;
But he'ld have faced a thousand such
Wild nights as thon, to see that smile
Again, and feel that tender touch
Upon his cheek.
                        'Twas well worth while
With such reward. And it was strange,
The difference such a little thing
Could make to them—how it could change
Their whole life for them, and could bring
Such happiness to them, though they
Had seemed as happy as could be
Before it came to them.
                              The day
Was shaping well. And there was she,
The lassie sleeping quietly
Within her arms, beside the gate.

The storm had split that lilac tree.
But he was tired, and it must wait.

MAKESHIFTS

A ND after all, 'twas snug and weather-tight,
His garret. That was much on such a night—
To be secure against the wind and sleet
At his age, and not wandering the street,
A shuffling, shivering bag-of-bones.

                                And yet
Things would be snugger if he could forget
The bundle of old dripping rags that slouched
Before him down the Canongate, that crouched
Close to the swing-doors of the Spotted Cow.
Why, he could see that poor old sinner now,
Ay! and could draw him, if he'd had the knack
Of drawing anything—a steamy, black
Dilapidation, basking in the glare,
And sniffing with his swollen nose in air
To catch the hot reek when the door swings wide
And shows the glittering paradise inside,
Where men drink golden fire on seats of plush
Lolling like gods: he stands there in the slush
Shivering, from squelching boots to sopping hat
One sodden clout, and blinking like a bat
Be-dazzled by the blaze of light: his beard
Waggles and drips from lank cheeks pocked and seared;
And the whole dismal night about him drips,
As he stands gaping there with watering lips
And burning eyes in the cold sleety drench,
Afire with thirst that only death may quench.

Yet he had clutched the sixpence greedily
As if sixpennyworth of rum maybe
Would satisfy that thirst. Who knows! It might
Just do the trick perhaps on such a night,
And death would be a golden, fiery drink
To that old scarecrow. 'Twould be good to think
His money'd satisfied that thirst, and brought
Rest to those restless fevered bones that ought
Long since to have dropped for ever out of sight.
It wasn't decent, wandering the night
Like that—not decent. While it lived it made
A man turn hot to see it, and afraid
To look it in the face lest he should find
That bundle was himself, grown old and blind
With thirst unsatisfied.
                              He'd thirsted, too,
His whole life long, though not for any brew
That trickled out of taps in gaudy bars
For those with greasy pence to spend!
                                        The stars
Were not for purchase, neither bought nor sold
By any man for silver or for gold.

Still, he was snug and sheltered from the storm.
He sat by his own hearth secure and warm,
And that was much indeed on such a night.
The little room was pleasant with the light
Glowing on lime-washed walls, kindling to red
His copper pots, and, over the white bed,
The old torn Rembrandt print to golden gloom.
'Twas much on such a night to have a room—
Four walls and ceiling storm-tight overhead.
Denied the stars—well, you must spend instead

Wilfrid Wilson Gibson

Your sixpences on makeshifts. Life was naught
But toiling for the sixpences that bought
Makeshifts for stars.

        'Twas snug to hear the sleet
Lashing the panes and sweeping down the street
Towards Holyrood and out into the night
Of hills beyond.   Maybe it would be white
On Arthur's seat to-morrow, white with snow—
A white hill shining in the morning glow
Beyond the chimney-pots, that was a sight
For any man to see—a snowy height
Soaring into the sunshine. He was glad,
Though he must live in slums, his garret had
A window to the hills.

        And he was warm,
Ay, warm and snug, shut in here from the storm.
The sixpences bought comfort for old bones
That else must crouch all night on paving-stones
Unsheltered from the cold.

        'Twas hard to learn
In his young days that this was life—to earn
By life-long labour just your board and bed—
Although the stars were singing overhead,
The sons of morning singing together for joy
As they had sung for every bright-eyed boy
With ears to hear since life itself was young—
And leave so much unseen, so much unsung.

He'd had to learn that lesson. 'Twas no good
To go star-gazing for a livelihood
With empty belly. Though he had a turn
For seeing things, when you have got to earn
Your daily bread first, there is little time
To paint your dream or set the stars to rhyme:

98

Wilfrid Wilson Gibson

Nay, though you have the vision and the skill
You cannot draw the outline of a hill
To please yourself, when you get home half-dead
After the day's work—hammers in your head
Still tapping, tapping
                              Always mad to draw
The living shape of everything he saw
He'd had to spend his utmost skill and strength
Learning a trade to live by, till at length
Now he'd the leisure the old skill was dead.

Born for a painter as it seemed, instead
He'd spent his life upholstering furniture.
'Twas natural enough men should prefer
Upholstery to pictures, and their ease
To little coloured daubs of cows and trees.
He didn't blame them, 'twas no fault of theirs
That they saw life in terms of easy chairs,
And heaven, like that old sinner in the slush,
A glittering bar upholstered in red plush.

'Twas strange to look back on it now, his life
His father, married to a second wife;
And home, no home for him since he could mind,
Save when the starry vision made him blind
To all about him, and he walked on air
For days together, and without a care
But as the years passed, seldomer they came
Those starry dazzling nights and days aflame,
And oftener a sudden gloom would drop
Upon him, drudging all day in the shop
With his young brother John—John always gay
Taking things as they came, the easy way,

Wilfrid Wilson Gibson

Not minding overmuch if things went wrong
At home, and always humming a new song

And then she came into his life, and shook
All heaven about him. He had but to look
On her to find the stars within his reach.
But, ere his love had trembled into speech,
He'd waked one day to know that not for him
Were those bright living eyes that turned dreams dim—
To know that while he'd worshipped, John and she
Had taken to each other easily . . .

But that was years ago . . . and now he sat
Beside a lonely hearth. And they were fat—
Ay, fat and old they were, John and his wife,
And with a grown-up family. Their life
Had not been over-easy: they'd their share
Of trouble, ay, more than enough to spare:
But they had made the best of things, and taken
Life as it came with courage still unshaken.
They'd faced their luck, but never gone half-way
To meet fresh trouble. Life was always gay
For them between the showers: the roughest weather
Might do its worst—they always stood together
To bear the brunt, together stood their ground
And came through smiling cheerfully. They'd found
Marriage a hard-up, happy business
Of hand-to-mouth existence more or less;
But taking all in all, well worth their while
To look on the bright side of things—to smile
When all went well, not fearing overmuch
When life was suddenly brought to the touch
And you'd to sink or swim. And they'd kept hold,

And even now, though they were fat and old
They'd still a hearty grip on life . . .
                                        They'ld be
Sitting there in their kitchen after tea
On either side the fire-place even now—
Jane with her spectacles upon her brow,
And nodding as she knitted, listening
While John, in shirt-sleeves, scraped his fiddle-string,
With one ear hearkening lest a foot should stop
And some rare customer invade the shop
To ask the price of that old Flanders' chest
Or oaken ale-house settle . . .
                                They'd the best
Of life, maybe, together . . .
                                And yet he—
Though he'd not taken life so easily,
Had always hated makeshifts more or less,
Grudging to swop the stars for sixpences,
And was an old man now, with that old thirst
Unsatisfied—ay, even at the worst
He'd had his compensations, now and then
A starry glimpse. You couldn't work with men
And quite forget the stars. Though life was spent
In drudgery, it hadn't only meant
Upholstering chairs in crimson plush for bars
Maybe it gave new meaning to the stars,
The drudgery, who knows!
                                At least the rare
Wild glimpses he had caught at whiles were there
Yet living in his mind. When much was dim
And drudgery forgotten, bright for him
Burned even now in memory old delights
That had been his in other days and nights.
He'd always seen, though never could express

Wilfrid Wilson Gibson

His eyes' delight, or only more or less:
But things once clearly seen, once and for all
The soul's possessions—naught that may befall
May ever dim, and neither moth nor rust
Corrupt the dream, that, shedding mortal dust,
Has soared to life and spread its wings of gold
Within the soul
               And yet when they were told,
These deathless visions, little things they seemed
Though something of the beauty he had dreamed
Burned in them, something of his youth's desire

And as he sat there, gazing at the fire—
Once more he lingered, listening in the gloom
Of that great silent warehouse, in the room
Where stores were kept, one hand upon a shelf,
And heard a lassie singing to herself
Somewhere unseen without a thought who heard,
Just singing to herself like any bird
Because the heart was happy in her breast,
As happy as the day was long. At rest
He lingered, listening, and a ray of light
Streamed from the dormer-window up a height
Down on the bales of crimson cloth, and lit
To sudden gold the dust that danced in it,
Till he was dazzled by the golden motes
That kept on dancing to those merry notes
Before his dreaming eyes, and danced as long
As he stood listening to the lassie's song . . .

Then once again, his work-bag on his back,
He climbed that April morning up the track
That took him by a short cut through the wood
Up to the hill-top where the great house stood,

Wilfrid Wilson Gibson

When suddenly beyond the firs' thick night
He saw a young fawn frisking in the light:
Shaking the dew-drops in a silver rain
From off his dappled hide, he leapt again
As though he'ld jump out of his skin for joy.
With laughing eyes light-hearted as a boy
He watched the creature unaware of him
Quivering with eager life in every limb,
Leaping and frisking on the dewy green
Beneath the flourish of the snowy gean,
While every now and then the long ears pricked
And budding horns, as he leapt higher, flicked
The drooping clusters of wild-cherry bloom,
Shaking the snow about him.   From the gloom
Of those dark wintry firs, his eyes had won
A sight of April sporting in the sun—
Young April leaping to its heart's delight
Among the dew beneath the boughs of white   .

And there'd been days among the hills, rare days
And rarer nights among the heathery ways—
Rare golden holidays when he had been
Alone in the great solitude of green
Wave-crested hills, a rolling shoreless sea
Flowing for ever through eternity—
A sea of grasses, streaming without rest
Beneath the great wind blowing from the west,
Over which cloud shadows sailed and swept away
Beyond the world's edge all the summer day.

The hills had been his refuge, his delight,
Seen or unseen, through many a day or night.
His help was of the hills, steadfast, serene

Wilfrid Wilson Gibson

In their eternal strength, those shapes of green
Sublimely moulded.
                    Whatsoever his skill,
No man hath ever rightly drawn a hill
To his mind—never caught the subtle curves
Of sweeping moorland with its dips and swerves—
Nor ever painted heather .
                    Heather came
Always into his mind like sudden flame,
Blazing and streaming over stony braes
As he had seen it on that day of days
When he had plunged into a sea of bloom,
Blinded with colour, stifled with the fume
Of sun-soaked blossom, the hot heady scent
Of honey-breathing bells, and sunk content
Into a soft and scented bed to sleep;
And he had lain in slumber sweet and deep,
And only wakened when the full moon's light
Had turned that wavy sea of heather white:
And still he'd lain within the full moon blaze
Hour after hour bewildered and adaze
As though enchanted—in a waking swoon
He'd lain within the full glare of the moon
Until she seemed to shine on him alone
In all the world—as though his body'd grown
Until it covered all the earth, and he
Was swaying like the moon-enchanted sea
Beneath that cold white witchery of light . .
And now, the earth itself, he hung in night
Turning and turning in that cold white glare
For ever and for ever . . .
                    She was there—
There at his window now, the moon. The sleet
And wind no longer swept the quiet street.

Wilfrid Wilson Gibson

And he was cold: the fire had burnt quite low ·
And, while he'd dreamt, there'd been a fall of snow.
He wondered where that poor old man would hide
His head to-night with thirst unsatisfied .

His thirst—who knows! but night may quench the thirst
Day leaves unsatisfied
                        Well, he must first
Get to his bed and sleep away the night,
If he would rise to see the hills still white
In the first glory of the morning light.

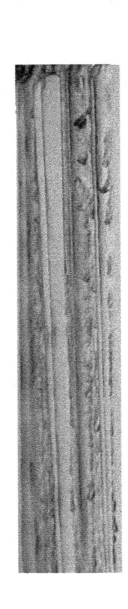

T. STURGE MOORE

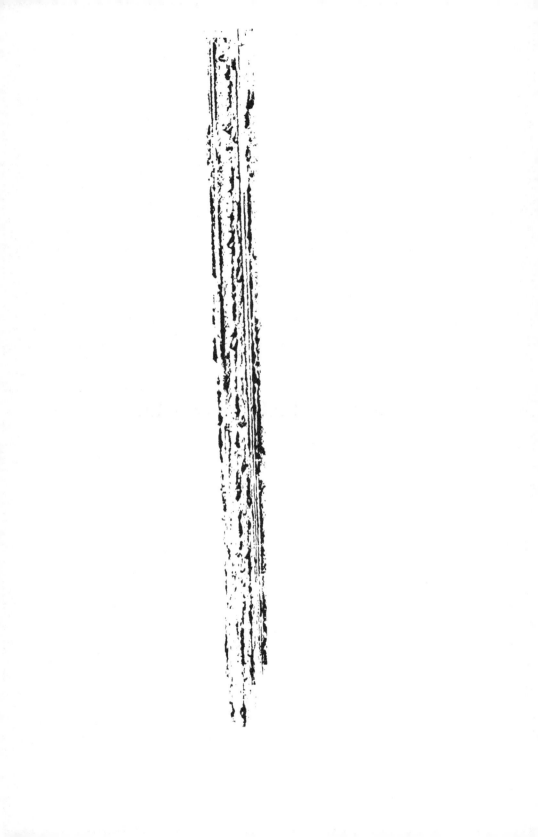

MICAH

IN Ephraim where skies are chiefly blue,
  Towards massive dome-like peaks the hills wind
    north.
The house of Micah on this ridge juts forth,
Some other roofs peep near, and rocks thrust through
Large leafy trees which shade an uphill road.
And all who pass wish his their own abode;
For hard thereby tufts of maidenhair fern
Kiss in a trough their green inverted showers,
And men, whose business presses, will waste hours
Watching each ripple flood the brim in turn.
The morning still felt fresh as it began
When thither came six hundred men of Dan;
From Eshtaol hailed some, from Zorah others;
And most were fully armed; for, near their brothers,
No longer was there place or land to till;
So they had sent forth five of might and skill
To search them out a vale for heritage.
These spies chose Laish; warless a long age
Its folk dwelt careless, as the manner holds
With the Zidonians, safe as sheep in folds,
Apart from all men else; in genial state
They pleased themselves without a magistrate
Who might put men to shame for doing wrong.
Those five now lead forth Dan, six hundred strong.
And having noted 'gainst the present day
What by the road most promised profit, they

T. Sturge Moore

Called a halt here,—not for that water's sake,
Nor to buy milk their children's fast to break:—
They had no honest cause to stop at all.
Though Micah's house stood back across a court
His Levite's lattice pierced the outer wall
And was the sooth- and charm-buyer's resort.
Talking they stopped; the priest was bound to hear,
His ears waked up by *Shibboleths*, full dear
Since Bethlehem his home bordered on theirs,
(Though he had not been near it now for years,
But, having found a place, he served this man
Who owned an house of gods). Those five of Dan,
Though they before had been his master's guests,
Now, while he questioned of those parts loved most,
Of all that, where he first was happy, rests,
Crossed the paved court, but did not hail their host;
Like boys who climb to where the wild hawk nests,
Neared hushed, and mute unto his God's house went.
His Ephod and the Teraphim which leant
By either post to guard the door they took;—
Glanced round like boys who for due vengeance look,
Dogged by dreamed whirr of wings;—bold then did
      seize,
Molten and graven, both his images.
This quickly done, they hastened to their friends.
And meanwhile Micah through his vineyard wends,
His mind unflecked by thought of guile or hate
To where his servants dig a goodly vat.
He means to see the floor well-grooved and flat.

"What do ye?" said the Levite at the gate.
The five made ready answer "Be thou dumb!
Lay thou thy hand upon thy mouth and come!
Shall we not need a father and a priest?

T. Sturge Moore

Whether is best for thee to serve one man
Or a whole tribe? Is the advantage least
Thou spiest with us?" Then in the midst of Dan,
Charged with the gods and ephod, pleased at once,
That Levite went. Putting their little ones,
Women and carts before them, all moved on.
Of Micah's maids no few watched what was done;
Who, when those men were not so nigh to hear,
Ventured beyond the threshold; wan with fear
Ran down among the vines and raised the cry
As then was wont; they pitched it shrill and high.

Listen! a thing of price
Is stolen—is lost—has gone!
He who to find it tries
Shall be well looked upon,—
He who will stop the thieves
His courage shall be showed!
Follow them by the shaking of the leaves—
Follow them by the dust above the road!
Gird on the sword—Take down the spear!
Ye who are not cowards—
Who own good names, who hold them dear—
An evil act is towards!
That workers of iniquity may tremble
Hither assemble!

Now Micah heard: and, conscious he was rich,
Harassed by shrewd surmises that would twitch
Its leading strings and bring his heart to stand,
Made toward the sound,—soon met a white-faced girl
Who gaped upon him, till his short command
Loosed her numb tongue and checked her senses' whirl
To pour his losses on him; though more fast
Her eyes outran her words, which being passed

T: Sturge Moore

Told what was known, yet only told it half.
Though Micah hurry, endless seems the path,
And countless are the incidents beheld;
His brain to trivial notice seems compelled.
Bronzed heads enquiring thrust out through green
      leaves—
The cloak which, to be going, some one heaves
About his shoulders, while he scowls to hear;
A spade struck deep in earth stands upright near;
Scared women's mantles flapping down the lanes;
The brisk commotion, as when summer rains
Set the farms bustling lest things hung to dry
Again be wetted,—so upon that cry
He saw men cross the open here and there,—
Not to take shelter. Matrons grave with care
Haste out of doors, not for white sheets distraught;
Lads keep pace with their elders, deep in thought;
A first time summoned at the public need
They pay example very anxious heed.
Grave for a sparkling cruelty returning,
Rapt students, they lack ears for questions wrung
From girls on whose words they had often hung—
Whose hearts now first are for an answer yearning,
Left thus among the children dazed with tears,
While baleful 'mid the leaves flash gathering spears.
At last was Micah thronged about with friends:
There in his own paved court all counsel bends
Unanimous in concert with his own,
As though four hundred limbs, not his alone
Answered his instincts, prompt, imperative,
For hot pursuit. One whom a host moves with,
The road glides past beneath him like a dream;
At length before his eyes in harness gleam
Six hundred men, and, bidden, lo, they wait:—

T₁ Sturge Moore

His voice, a hundredfold its volume now,
So wields control. Majestic to dictate,
Moved forth before his friends, rebukes to bow
The minds of robbers throng into his thoughts:
He stands to choose before their ranked cohorts.
A mocking voice intrudes,—" What aileth thee?
Why comest thou with such a company?"
Then Micah gasps: " My gods ye have taken away,
Both which I made; the priest he too is gone;
What have I more? Am I then wondered on
Coming amongst you? How is it? Ye say
' What aileth thee?' "—" We, if you must know why,
Are six to one." In feigned concern some cry,
" Let not thy voice be heard amongst us, lest
Some angry fellows run upon thee, then
Thou mightest lose thy life; yea, thou wert best,
For sake of these thy household, with young men
To hold thy peace, since such have froward wills,
And crying oft provoketh further ills."
Micah must turn; they are too strong for him,
And, round him turning, hills, trees, neighbours swim.
They led him home: he heard each kind friend's word,
Yet seemed to them as though he hardly heard.
The hill was steep to climb again, and high
The sun rode; earth was baked; his mouth was dry.
The dust in the deep ruts felt soft as mud;
A hush lay on the country; chewing cud,
The cattle kept the shade; and dotted trees
On distant hills did still as rocks remain;
For, void of breath and destitute of ease,
No hint that God was moving gave the plain.
His mother came to meet him; she was kind;
His woe more than their loss distressed her mind.
She led him in, spoke something, touched his sleeve;

And every act brought a minute reprieve
From that too present blank crushed on his sense.
Micah must from the poor receive an alms,
Ere life's jammed movements regain due suspense;
What servants do helps more than costly balms.
To watch the swallows if the eye be caught
Sufficient proves to slack the bonds of thought.
The rich indeed few turns of fate can bless,
Yet many leave those who own much with less.
When put to native poverty again
Men hardy-to-feel-rich must pay dire toll;
Their thriftless thrift results in abject pain.
Than such a man it takes a wealthier soul
To count with loss. Above the Promised Land,
Though it lie distant, let but Moses stand
And see—forbidden entrance,—he is blest,
And angels lay him quite content to rest.
" Since I have seen thy face let me now die "
Said Israel to Joseph; listen why.
" Because thou art alive still whom I wept
And mourned for dead." Such airy food has kept
The strong soul fine; possession were too much:
Since mind conceives, why should the coarse hand touch?

His gods had still less power in Micah's breast
Than in the world, so on his mind scorn pressed
With " Lords, though eyed with jasper, who are kind
And cruel fickly, might as well be blind.
What, do these chaunting women gain relief,
While I who wealth have lavished ache in grief!
Dumb is my woe, but theirs with words is fed
Copiously gushing as for strong man dead : "—

" Wail, O nest of eagles young !
Since those are now taken away

Tɩ Sturge Moore

Who nursed ye, on the hill-crest hung,
Cry out, bestir, and clamour with the tongue
For this fair-shining is a cruel day!

" How shall henceforth any know
Surely of the coming rain?
When the seed 'twere best to sow,
Now or not yet? What will show?
Things when lost must aye remain
In the corner where they rolled
Even should they be of gold.
Ailing babes will wail in vain,
Will pine, will perish ;—watched, not helped in pain.

" Weep, for the Ephod is gone!
To us it no more will give
Urim nor Thummim; but on
Our eyes night drops; we live
Henceforth as the blind, we cry—
Like little foxes from holes
When their mother is fast in the snare—
We cry—but what help is there?
Great silence o'erwhelms our souls.

" Man's words in this strange world no more avail
Than in our midst the new-born child's sad wail.
Thus ringed by elder natures must we weep;
Though Thunder speak, the thought is passing deep.
And who can read the faces of the clouds
Or penetrate the mystery that shrouds
The placid smiling of the sky?
Then lift ye up the voice and cry!
Our Gods perchance may hear—
They yet are somewhat near.

For if they turn not back ye are forlorn;
Midnight is silent and the Noon;
Who shall whisper with the Morn?
With the Evening who commune?
These counsel with themselves alone—
To no man is their favour shown.
Then cry aloud, be urgent in your wail;
When all else fails, persistence may avail."

All round him rose a coolness of stone walls;
Translucent vine-leaves softly laced the glare
Which else had trespassed through the portal deep.
Along the walls stood vintage of old years
In massive jars high as a woman's chin,
A thick dust mantling each round-shouldered well.
Bundles of herbs, baskets and pruning hooks,
Hung from the cedarn rafters, vague in gloom;
And on the smooth-planed table there was fruit—
Damsons and pears,—while, from its trencher, sliced
A crusted melon, luscious womb of seeds,
Glowed and shed fragrance. Audible, since they
Have ceased to sing, the gurgling spring tunes time,
And keeps in mind the cavernous cool rocks,
Umbrageous trees, and many a hazy glimpse
Across the basking plains, whereto his vines
Slope with their mellow ranks of rustling leaves.
But 'mid the little chapel's hollow walls
Now dwells an aching absence where his gods
Had stood in glimmering splendour to protect,
For ever smiling on a pile of gifts—
Crisp flowery loaves and golden maize and doves,
Grey doves with yellow plumage round their necks,
With ribbed feet tied, drooped wings and blue veiled
        eyes.

T. Sturge Moore

No more will some two hundred kneel for awe,
No shout of praise start every rock to tell,
And loudly tell, Jehovah's glorious name;
Nor will he joy in prestige erewhile his,—
A rich and envied god-possessing man.

Beyond his fathers wise, he had had suck
Of all the abundance which in seas is found,
And of the treasures hidden in the sand.
Close speech with swarthy captains had he held,
And placed much confidence in ships; yet kept
Well-watered vineyards, sounding fields of corn.
His beard was black; still hale and firm his limbs;
The fuller's finest white with scarlet fringe
He wore, and it became him; chains of gold
At feast and wedding jangled on his breast;
Damsels still met him blushing —younger men
Passed for less handsome. What harsh climax now
Crowned his content? the gratitude of Gods,
Whose images, made from his mother's gold,
He honoured,—and was honoured in return,
Till now, he thought. Yet still the thunder failed
To bring their state home; wrathful agencies
Muttered not, mustering round the massive forms
Of Ebal and of Gerizim. His wife
And mother only dream of succour now.
Yes, they are cooking: from the further room
Come and return; they sigh, but taste the broth,
And know how much salt lacks. Trivial concern
Divides their hearts with woe: life's menials they,
Incapable of concentrated aim.
They grudge to risk their wealth on Tyrian trade;
And when they see it doubled, "Praise the Lord!"
Appropriate seems to them. But men face risk,

Can calculate and gain; therefore to them
Loss is calamity; girls buoyed on chance
Have not the strength to feel. And yet he went,
When told the supper waited him above.

The roof of that tall house lightly was raised
On slender colonnettes set nigh as close
As palings: Micah through their intervals
Had oft at leisure from his couch surveyed
The plain stretched round him; slingers in the corn;
The wine-press whither they bring in his grapes:
Unmuzzled and well-fed, slow oxen trod
The terrace threshing-floor. His children near
Played on all fours; his wife would bend her down
To kiss him, having crooned some song he loved.
And still to-day his eyes are fond enough
To rest upon the hills, to weigh the worth
Of this year's vintage, watch the labourers' heads
Appear and disappear beyond the brink
Of his new vat: languidly stray his eyes;
Anon he finds them choosing from the meats.
His palate next approves: his lips return
His mother's smile. Yet is his good soul hurt
At every acquiescence: yet less hurt
Each time; and so he slips into fond ease,
Half conscious of some failure, discontent
To be content. The long day closes in,
And on the cooing dove-cot comes a lull;
The night wind whispers o'er the corn; the pipe
Of some boy goat-herd reedlike from the cliffs
Trembles and dies away. He seeks his bed.
And as a girl who quits her home to serve
In some rich house, and wear far gayer clothes,
(Dance, song, and work with beads, henceforth her tasks)

Heart-broken feels when first she hears that news;
Yet presently the talk and bustle scare
Her sorrow till she smiling takes her leave:—
So Micah, quit of all deep feeling, smiled;
And, to the sound of water gurgling o'er
Its vaulted rocky well, entered on realms
Of slumber soother than the world. But as
Mid those less strenuous days a sense of loss
Returns upon that girl, bewild'ring, fraught
With blunt remorse, indefinite rebuke,
And makes her sob in bed at night,—so now
Into his first light sleep, disquiet crept:—
As when the night wind comes across the sea,
Sweeps through the halls and markets and dense streets
That crowd a haven, steady and cold and salt:
Drives forth foul odours, penetrates dark dens,
To wearied slaves brings sleep, to fevered death:—
Shakes the low tavern door—ends the carouse
Of drunken sailors, blowing out their lamp,
And moaning with the voice of comrades drowned:—
So now through Micah's brain discomfort came,
Salt as with tears and set one way like wind,
Drove through him, roused compunction for the pain
Deserted with such ease, jostled bland dreams
As serried soldiers elbow through the throngs
Of chatty market folk; and no man knows
Aught of their orders, though all dread to learn
Whether some heavier tax be levied now—
Corvée exacted on some boast in stone—
Or whether their king's mind has taken late
A sanguinary ply, because in sleep
He hears a long blade on a smooth wet stone
Pass and re-pass; and then a silence falls
As though who whets it, curious of the edge,

Slipped it along his thumb and smiled—but soon
Recurs the regular lisp 'twixt steel and stone.
Loud Micah's heart beat as men's then will beat—
Guessed at a wrath no more to be forestalled
Than such a fear-besotted tyrant's rage—
Stopped dead as their hearts stop when all at once
The trumpets snarl ear-splitting o'er the booths.
It was as though a thunder pealed him words:—
"Shall gods depart, yet be so briefly mourned?"
Then, compassed round with cloud, the cherubim
Bowed with the heavens and came down, while he
Cowered and kept his face pressed on the dust,
Expecting death: but ah! they turned their wheels
Which did not crunch across his abject corse,
Yet rumbled near, continuing less loud
Until they passed from ear-shot. Long he ached
In pulseless silence and black void.
                                    A child
Abandoned in the dark begins to wail,—
Then, panic-goaded, daring never stop,
In one continuous scream throws back its head,
And seeks to drive life's self forth with the sound,
Till suffocated, stunned, faint, it must lie
And cough. So Micah dreamed he did, and heard—
After interminable flagging throbs—
His mother move from near him with a lamp
And say: "He sleeps again," pause and then add
"He breatheth quietly; come, leave him now!"
Hot with strange shame, grown man with child confused,
Some time elapsed ere he became aware
That, round the chamber where his bed was set,
Rain made such sound as when it long hath rained.

R. C. TREVELYAN

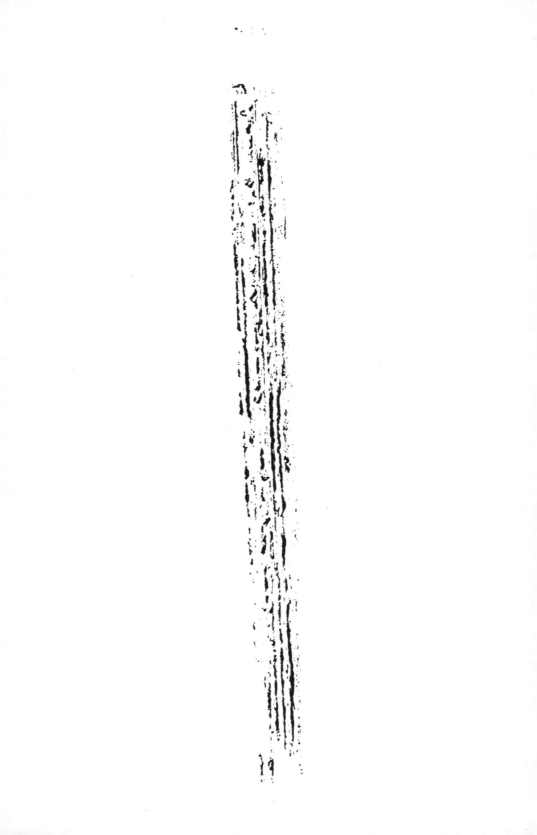

R. C. Trevelyan

THE PEARL TREE

KRISHNA
RADHA
YASHÒDA .   .   .   .   .   *Krishna's mother*
A RISHI .   .   .   .   .   *an aged ascetic*
VALARÀMA .   .   .   .   *Krishna's brother*
SUDÀMA .   .   .   .   *a herd-boy*
LÀLITA .   .   .   *a Gopi maiden, friend of Radha*
CHANDRÀVALI .   .   .   .   *a Gopi maiden*
COWHERD BOYS .   .   .   *comrades of Krishna*
GOPI MAIDENS .   .   .   *companions of Radha*
APSÀRAS .   .   .   *celestial dancing maidens*
A NEIGHBOUR OF YASHODA

The Scene is the village of Gokula, and the jungle of Vrindàvan upon the banks of the Jumna.

SCENE I

Y<small>ASHODA</small> *is standing at the entrance of her house with a stick in her hand. In front of her is a crowd of some dozen herd-boys.*

Boys.

M OTHER Yashoda! Mother Yashoda!
    Yashoda. Go away, bad boys! Go away!
Boys. Mother Yashoda, give us our Krishna!
Yashoda. Go away, or I'll fetch my stick.
And you, Valarama, come in with you quick.

123

R. C. Trevelyan

Didn't I say that Krishna and you
Were not to go out to the jungle to-day?
Boys. Mother Yashoda, we want our Krishna.
The time is come for our sport and play.
The cows are lowing, the sky is blue;
The Vrinda meadows are fresh with dew.
We must be going, and Krishna too.
Make him ready to come with us.
Yashoda.   Nay!
Krishna must bide at home to-day.
Valarama. But why, mother, why?
Yashoda. He's ill in bed with a shivering fever.
Valarama. Oh, what a lie!
Yashoda.   So make no noise,
For he's just gone to sleep.
Valarama.   Don't you believe her.
Yashoda. Begone, or you'll wake him, you ragamuffin
        boys.   [*A flute is heard from within the house.*
Boys. Listen! Oh, that is his flute. Clear and gay
He pipes, " to the meadows away, away!"
Silly little mother, will you tell us still
That our darling Krishna's asleep or ill?
Yashoda. Sick or sound, he shall bide at home.
Never again with you shall he roam,
Tearing his clothes at wrestling and racing,
Risking his neck up monkey-chasing,
(Yes, I know all your madcap pranks,)
Diving down from Jumna's banks
Into crocodile pools. No, no, little fools,
Henceforth he bides with me at home.
Boys. How cross and stupid these grown-up folks are!
Come, we must sing our very best to coax her.
Listen awhile, we pray,
Mother Yashoda dear.

Give us our Krishna for this one day,
This one day in the whole long year.
Nothing is there for you to fear:
For of him we will take great care.
In the midst of us all shall he go like a king.
We will carry his flute and his staff.
So merry is Krishna, as a bird on the wing,
That he dances along as he goes.
If thorny or rough be the path,
On our shoulders high will we carry him.
When the sun's rays grow too strong,
To a tree's cool shadow will we lead him.
There shall he rest, while we how best
To please him strive. But if perchance,
Tired with frolic, faint from the dance,
We see him pale, with wild-wood fruits
And berries will we feed him.
Yashoda. And poison him too: yes, that would you do.
Go, you scamps, go.
Boys. Poison our darling Krishna! No!
We can tell good from evil fruit
As well as any root-fed Rishi can do.
Give us our Krishna, Yashoda dear.
If he come not with us to-day,
If we hear not the sound of his flute,
How shall we dance and be gay?
The peacock, the cuckoo, the bee,
And the squirrel high up in the banyan tree
Are waiting and listening with eager ear
To catch the sound of his pipings.
If we haven't our Krishna, whose dark hair
Shall we crown with peacock plumes, and deck
With bright wild flowers?
We will make him sit in the midst of us

R. C. Trevelyan

Under the cool Kadamva bowers,
And pipe to us, while we
Wreathe him a garland for his neck
Of champak blossoms and all gay flowers
That in Vrinda's groves and meadows be,
On stalk or tree,
Malaka, Kunda and Madhavi.
Then suffer him, mother, to go.
If they see not his sweet face,
The cows will not drink or graze.
If they hear not Krishna's flute,
They will not so much as low,
But will stand like carved things mute.
Your son, little mother, has magic arts.
All things that have ears and hearts,
Silly cattle and beasts and men,
When they hear his pipe, must obey his will:
In his music is such sweet force.
Saintliest Yogis of jungle and hill
See their holiest visions then;
And the Jumna stays in her course.
Yashoda. Spare your song. Though all day long
You stand here begging, you won't coax me,
For all your noise, to let him go free,
You good-for-nothing boys.
Boys. [*Making a rush for the door, and trying to force
        their way past* YASHODA *into the house.*]
Then we must take him; and away we'll go,
Whether his mother may wish it or no.
In at the door like a swarm
Of angry bees we'll storm.
Let her scold and stamp and tear her hair,
We won't care.
Yashoda.   Wicked boys, do you dare!

Away with you, thieves, or you'll taste my stick.
Ho, neighbours, neighbours! hither! come quick!
They would carry my Krishna away.
Boys. Krishna! Krishna! We can't get through:
Her stick's so thick. Oh, what shall we do?
Must we go without you to-day?

> [*During the scuffle* KRISHNA *climbs out unnoticed
> through a window at the side, and standing
> behind the boys, sets his flute to his lips and
> plays a few notes.*

Boys. Hark! His flute! Oh see, that's he!
Krishna! Krishna!

> [*They rush back to where* KRISHNA *is standing.*

Away to the jungle—away, away!
Silly little mother, goodbye, goodbye!
Catch us if you can in the trees so high.
We'll teach you to climb. Come try, come try.

> [KRISHNA *and the* Boys *run off together in the
> direction of the jungle.*

Yashoda. Krishna, you cruel boy, come back! They're
   gone; they're out of earshot,
Off to the jungle bounding like a pack of pelted
   monkeys.

Enter NEIGHBOUR.

Neighbour. Yashoda, what's the matter? What meant
   all that hurley-burly?
Yashoda. It was those wicked cowherd boys: they've
   stolen away my Krishna,
To the jungle—yes, and I've no more the legs or breath
   to chase them.
Neighbour. Why, mother, is your Krishna still an in-
   fant in the cradle,

R. C. Trevelyan

That you should swaddle him up at home, and keep him
    from his playmates?
Yashoda. Do you not know how all his life demons
    and evil yakshas
Have sought to lure him within their power, to kidnap
    or destroy him?
Neighbour. So far it seems your Krishna's proved a
    match for all these demons.
Take my advice and pray to Vishnu. He'll be the lad's
    best keeper.   [*Exit* NEIGHBOUR.
Yashoda. Vishnu! To him how oft have I not prayed?
But who knows when the Gods have heard? 'Tis said,
Ofttimes like men they sleep, or sit and watch
Apsaras dancing. How then should they catch
The sighs of us poor mortals? And they tell
How from their heavens the Gods descend and dwell
Within the bodies of wild beasts and men.
Can they have ears to listen to us then?
Those boys spoke true: my son has magic arts;
Or why should he have such power over all hearts?
I sometimes think, so different he seems
From all else, that a God's soul, in its dreams,
Oft enters him, and lodges there awhile.
Did not sage Rishis journey mile on mile
To behold him in his cradle, and bow low
Worshipping him with gifts and prayers, as though
He were indeed a great God visiting us?
But I am not so vain and credulous
As to believe all the fine tales and lies
These Yogis cheat us with to win more rice.
Well, when my household tasks are done, I'll go
To fetch him home, be he a God or no.
                [*She goes into the house.*

R. C. Trevelyan

SCENE II

The Vrinda Forest, near the banks of the Jumna. Under the broad shade of a peepul tree sits an aged RISHI, *in an attitude of tranced meditation.*

Krishna.

WHEN she smiles, how beautiful is my Radha;
　　When like clear skies after rain
Her eyes are filled with laughter again,
And shyly gazing into mine
Seem to plead:
" Ask not why so early from my comrades
I stole away; ask not why so bright
Yon moon is rising, nor for whom to-night
My loveliness is more lovely:
Only come, come now to the jungle with me,
Krishna, my playmate."

Ah but then most beautiful is my Radha,
When her scornfully flashing eyes
Mock me as lightning from dark skies.
Then deeply beyond their anger and disdain
Gazing, there I read
All that within her heart is lurking,
In secret working unconfessed,
Hope and wistful fear and yearning pain,
Innocent tenderness, reluctant
Proud hesitation and wayward guile.
Then my heart leaps joyfully, like a mother's,
When her child turns gravely from her breast,

And gazing upward into her eyes, the first time
Kindles answering smile for smile.

[*He now notices the* RISHI.

What is this? Who is here?
Some saintly Rishi lapsed in trance. More still
He seems than a deserted ant-hill, and
As void perchance of any thought or joy.
Vishnu preserve me from such torpid saintliness!
Yet have I heard men say that when the mind
And bodily senses sleep, the wakeful soul
Delightedly goes forth and wandering sees
Visions divine and glorious, unbeheld
By mortals else. If that be so, maybe
Were I to waken now within my flute
A solemn yet a rapturous melody,
Who knows but it may open wide the gate
Of Indra's Paradise to this poor Yogi,
And bathe his parching spirit a brief while
In rivers of living joy?

[*He plays a melody on his flute. The music
gradually rouses the* RISHI *from his trance.*
KRISHNA *stops playing; and the* RISHI,
who, though now fully awake, does not see
KRISHNA, *speaks with his hands joined in
adoration.*

Rishi. Vishnu! Almighty Vishnu!
To thee be praise!
Among the Gods in Swarga have I been.
Yet at first I saw there
Gloom only and despair;
And a voice I heard that cried:
" Where is our Vishnu, where? "
And at that word
I saw Gods shudder and turn pale,

130

And heard the Apsaras and Ghandavas wail:
The Heavens grew dark, and all awhile sat mute:
When from afar was heard
The faint note of a flute,
More near, more near, till in the midst there stood
A youth, a shepherd boy, who played
Such melodies on his flute as made
The eyes of Gods grow dim,
And their hearts marvellously set free
To wander forth delightedly
From their grief-gloomed selves to him,
Where his slender limbs to the music swayed.
Listening and beholding then
All knew him, the beloved, the adored
Of Gods and mortal men,
Their Vishnu, to their sight restored.
But the flute ceased, and a change came,
And the dream of bliss was ended:
For the light of Heaven darkened,
As away the vision faded.
Grief-consumed and again bereft
Of him they loved were the Gods left.
I too wake to the world's woe.

> [KRISHNA *sounds his flute again; the* RISHI
> *looks up and sees him, then falls at his
> feet, worshipping him.*

Ah!—The flute!
It is He!
Krishna. Good Yogi, rise. Where are your wits astray,
That you should take me for a God to worship?
Rishi. Art thou not then . . . .?
Krishna.   Yes! Who I am, you know.
Rishi. Who art thou? I am old: my sight is dim.
Krishna. I am Krishna, Nanda and Yashoda's son.

R. C. Trevelyan

Rishi. Krishna, my child, was it thy flute I heard?
Krishna. My flute it was. Good Rishi, I did ill
If by my foolish pipings your deep thoughts
And saintly meditations were disturbed.
Rishi. Nay, child, but there was magic in thy flute:
How else should I have seen what I have seen?
Twenty years in this forest have I dwelt;
But never yet, fast and afflict my body
Austerely as I might, could I attain
True vision of the Gods until this hour.
Blest be thy flute, and the lips that played thereon.
Boys. [*Without.*] Krishna! Where are you hiding?
    Krishna!
Krishna. Hark! they are coming. They've followed
    the flute.
Old man, now mind: not a word to them of me!
Not a nod! Keep still and mum as a root.
Goodbye! Now for this peepul tree!
       [KRISHNA *climbs up quickly into the peepul tree.*
        The RISHI *resumes his attitude of medita-*
        tion.

Enter VALARAMA, SUDAMA, SUBALA, *and the other herd*
    boys, running.

Boys. Krishna! Krishna!
Sudama. This way! It was here I heard it last.
Valarama. Hi! not so fast! It's just such a place
He'd choose to hide in.
Subala.   Oh what a shame
To lead us such a chase!
Where in the world has he got to?
He's always up to some trick or other.
Valarama, you're his brother:
It's for you to tell him not to.

132

Valarama. I'm not to blame. Haven't I done so
A thousand times? But it 's all the same:
It 's never any use.
Sudama.   Come, why should we run so?
If he wants to tease, why play his game?
Look, there 's the old Yogi.
Another Boy.   Yogi, please,
Has Krishna been your way?
Another. Have you seen him atall to-day?
Another. Is he hiding among those trees?
Wont you give us a word or a nod?
Another. Give him a prod. He cant have heard.
Another. It 's no use : leave him. He hasn't a word
For anyone less than a God.
Sudama. Come, let 's sit down and cool ourselves under
    this shady peepul.
See here the grass is fresh and soft, the very place for
    dozing.
It 's full noon now, and all the birds are silent save the
    kokilas.
Let Krishna play at hide and seek alone, if he 's a mind to.
Subala. Maybe it 's Radha and the Gopis he 's playing
    hide and seek with.
Another Boy. Well, be his game whate'er it may, why
    should we fash to find him?
Sudama. Still, I *do* wish we had him here. One feels so
    dull without him.
What shall we do to pass the time?
Valarama.   Why, sleep.
Sudama.   But I'm not sleepy.
Come, someone, tell us a story, do, of Rama or of Shiva.
                              [*A silence.*
How is it that we miss him so? It 's no use our pre-
    tending·

When he's away one feels as cross and stupid as a
    buffalo.   [*A silence.*

Subala. Where are the cows? They must be lost. Well
    now there'll be some trouble.

It's Krishna's fault. When we missed *him*, of course
    we quite forgot *them*.

Another Boy. Look, there they come. Count them,
    Sudama. My counting stops at twenty.

Sudama. They're all there, the whole thirty-six; even
    Draupadi, the lame one.

Look at them. Aren't they a lovely sight. No girls
    are half so pretty.

Yet girls wear bangles, ear-rings, chains of pearls or
    gold and silver;

While cows wear nothing, or at best some miserable
    necklace

Of blue and yellow beads. Just think; if we could only
    make them

A necklace each of pearls, how fine and beautiful they'ld
    look then!

Valarama. Yes, they'ld look fine no doubt. But how
    do you propose, Sudama,

To find your pearls? If you expect to pick them from
    a pearl-bush,

I'm thinking you may have to plant one first.

Sudama.   Well, since they aren't stones,

They must grow somewhere, I suppose: else how
    should the girls come by them?

Valarama. They're bought at fairs for cowries.

Sudama.   Yes, but how do the shopmen get them?

If only Krishna now were here, I'm certain he would
    teach us

How to make pearls as fast as clouds pelt hail-stones
    when it thunders.

R. C. Trevelyan

Krishna. [*From above in the peepul tree.*] Sudama!
Sudama.   That's his voice. Where are you, Krishna?
Look, there he sits, up in the peepul tree!
Krishna. Go now, Sudama:
Haste back to the village as my messenger
To Radha. Say: Krishna has need of one
Small pearl, one only, from her ears or neck.
This pearl, if she will grant it, he will sow,
And from it raise more than a thousand-fold,
To deck with pearls the dewlaps of our cows.
Say also that her gift shall be repaid
Many times over both in pearls and thanks.
Sudama. But, Krishna, do you really mean to send me
        on such an errand?
They'll mock me and make me seem a fool, those Gopi
        girls, I know it.
Krishna. Do as I bid you. Linger not, but go.
Valarama.   How now, Sudama!
Afraid of Radha and the girls?
Sudama.   Well, you go, Valarama,
Since you're so brave.
Valarama.   Oh no; it's you we've always
        thought the hero.
Sudama. Well, go I must, though I don't want to, since
        so Krishna wills it.   [*Exit* SUDAMA.
Subala. Valarama, tell me, (don't speak loud), would
        you yourself have liked it,
If Krishna had chosen to send *you* on such a senseless
        errand?
Valarama. No indeed. And I'm wondering too, if Radha
        now should lend him
This pearl, what Krishna would do then, except look
        mighty foolish.
Sow pearls indeed! Who ever heard such nonsense!

135

Krishna. [*From above.*]   Valarama!
The rest shall have twelve pearls apiece; you only six,
and small ones.

SCENE III

*The village of Gokula. Lalita, Chandravali and several
other of the Gopi maidens are sitting in the shade of
a banyan tree, watching Radha, who is seated some-
what apart from her companions, absorbed in her own
thoughts.*

Chandravali. [*Singing.*]
"Now may I go?"
        "Ah, no, no! Not yet!" I sighed.
"The hour is come.
May I now go?"
Grief held me dumb.
"May I go now?"
He whispered thrice,
Ere I replied,
"Go, my love, since it must be so."
One step he made,
Then turned to look
Deep in my eyes:
Within his hands my hands he took,
And bade me vow:
"Though now we part,
Yet from my heart,
O my love, thou
Canst never go."

Lalita. She does not hear you, Chandra.
Still she sits staring on the trees,

136

R. C. Trevelyan

Dreaming with open eyes.
Radha!
Will nothing wake her?
Chandravali.   She must be bewitched.
Lalita. Well, if she be, we know by whom. His name
Perchance may rouse her. I will try.
Chandravali.   No, no!
It will but anger her.
Lalita.   What if it do?
That would be better than this love-sick moping.

[*She sings.*] Oh ye who say:
" Forget him. Hath he not forgotten thee? "
How am I to forget?
Did I not offer him my soul in play?
Did it not fly to him like a bird
By a fowler's piping lured,
And perch upon a tree,
And sing to him? till he
Like a fowler caught it in his net,
And keeps it captive yet.

Now in his cage he bears me all day long.
To my sweet song he pays no heed.
Not though I starve for it, one small seed
Of pity has he granted me as yet.
Soon shall I perish. Then alone,
When thought and memory are flown,
Dying forgotten shall I forget thee, Krishna.

Radha. Lalita! what do you mean?
You know that name is hateful to me.
Lalita.   Hateful?
It was not always so.
Radha. Oh, you are pert and sly. Leave me in peace.

Lalita. I had hoped to please your mood: but I mistook.
I ought to have remembered:
That name was hateful to you: yes.
But listen now: I'll make amends.

[*She sings.*] O ye maidens of Vrindavan, heed my warn-
ing; do not wander
Down yon pathway to the jungle, lest you meet with
such mischance
As of late befell me there.
Pleasant are the groves of Vrinda; yet in their cool
shades there lurks
A monster, a dread king of Nagas. Deadly is the very
glance
Of those bright eyes. Oh beware!
Yes beware, for he is gentle: winsome is his shape and
lovely
His poised head; his every motion lures and charms:
yea, his the art
To entice and to betray.
Ere thou art aware his swiftly gliding coils are round
thee twining,
And the poison from his deadly kiss is burning up the
heart
Of the serpent Krishna's prey.
    [RADHA *rises in anger and walks away.*
Chandravali. Oh, you are cruel, Lalita.
See, she is hurt. You have driven her away.

Enter SUDAMA. *He stands hesitating, and looks shyly
round him at the* Gopis.

Lalita. Why, there's Sudama. Look at him how he
gapes

And stares around him like a duck new-hatched!
Whom do you seek, Sudama?
Sudama.   I want Radha.
Where is she?
Chandravali.   There she comes. You'd best beware.
She'll bite your head off, if you come from Krishna.
Sudama. Vishnu protect me! How she glares! Oh why
Did Krishna send me here with this fool's message?
Lalita. Radha, here is Sudama come to speak with you.
Radha. [*Who has returned.*] Well!—Speak! Why do
     you gape upon me?
Sudama. Krishna sent me . . .
Radha. [*Turning to go.*]   Krishna!
Lalita. But you *must* stay and hear him.
Radha.   Well, what is it?
Sudama. Krishna sent me to ask of you a pearl,
Just one pearl from your necklace or your ears .
Lalita. What should he want a pearl for?
Sudama.   For our cows;
To make pearl-strings to hang their dewlaps with.
Chandravali. And pray, what use would one pearl be
     for that?
Sudama. He means, you see, to plant it in the ground .
One of the Girls. And then?
Sudama. Then it will grow to a pearl-tree, so he hopes.
The Girls. [*Laughing.*] A pearl-tree!
Sudama. He says besides, he will pay Radha back
Many times over both in pearls and thanks.
Radha. Go to your Krishna: take this answer back.
Know that pearls grow in sea-shells, not on trees;
That they are precious things, not like the flowers
You pluck in Vrinda's forests every day.
A notion so extravagant, tell him, please,

Is worthy only of an ignorant,
Stupid, unreasoning cowherd, like himself.
What! adorn cows with necklaces of pearl!
Could even the most lavish rajah on earth
Conceive so crazed a fancy. Tell him this
Moreover, that once every year by night
From Svati's constellation there descends
Into each destined shell a mystic ray
Of fertilizing light: and thus it is
Are formed those pearls that divers risk their lives
To fetch from the sea's depth. Let him not deem
That pearls are things easy and cheap to win
Like a kadamva or a champak flower.
The Girls. Well done, Radha!—Look how he stands
Gaping and blushing and blinking!
His crook slips out of his hands.
Krishna will hardly be pleased, I'm thinking,
With such an answer as that.
But his message was nothing but impudent fooling;
So it's all fair tit for tat.
If the laugh's gone against him, he deserves his
    schooling.
Mind, Sudama, you don't forget
One word of what Radha said.
Pearls grow on sea-shells, not on trees.
Pearls are not champak buds, nor yet
Any kind of flower, whether white or red,
Pink, yellow or blue. Remember too,
Svati's the name of the constellation
Whose love-beams quicken the oyster nation.
Fix that in your memory, please.
                    [SUDAMA *retires in confusion.*

Radha. Lalita!
Lalita. Yes, Radha!

Radha. Hasten, Lalita. Follow behind Sudama:
Keep hidden among the trees: note all he says
To Krishna, and how Krishna answers him:
Is he angry, or seems vexed, or does but laugh.
Bring me back word of all he says and does.
Quick now; but be not seen.
Lalita.   Trust me for that.
Radha. But haste.
Lalita. [*Aside.*]   Ah, Radha, never could you hide
Your love-sick thoughts from me, for all your pride.
                                                              [*Exit* LALITA.

SCENE IV

The same as Scene II. The RISHI *is still sitting under
the peepul tree.* KRISHNA *and the* herd-boys *are
lying or sitting idly on the grass here and there.*
SUDAMA *stands before* KRISHNA. LALITA *crouches in
hiding behind a bush, watching and listening.*

Krishna.

RADHA spoke so, Sudama?
    Sudama.   Yes, just so.
Krishna. Unreasoning? Ignorant? She spoke those
        words?
Sudama. Those were her very words: I am quite sure.
Lalita. [*Aside.*] Ignorant, stupid, and unreasoning;
Yes, and a cowherd too.
Krishna. She will be sorry for them soon perhaps.
Sudama. What will you do now, Krishna? Our fine plan
Is spoilt, it seems, without a pearl to plant.
Valarama. He does look vexed. Best let him be awhile.
I've never seen him so put out before.

Subala. Small wonder too, after her shrewd reply.
Oh, you can see it's not the pearl so much,
As Radha's scorn. That's touched him to the quick.
Valarama. If I'd been Radha, I'ld have sent the pearl.
He'ld look more foolish then than he does now.
Sudama. Dont be so sure. It's my belief that Radha
Will yet feel sorry she tried to mock our Krishna.
Lalita. [*Aside.*] Then Radha will be changed.
Radha was never sorry.

Enter YASHODA.

Yashoda. Krishna, where are you? Krishna! Krishna!
A Boy.　　　　　　What's that? Why, it's Yashoda.
Yashoda. Ah, now I've found you, wicked boys.
A Boy.　　　　　　Yes, now there'll be some trouble.
Yashoda. Come home at once. How dare you play the
　　　　truant from your mother,
And make her run through hissing snakes and tigers
　　　　hither to fetch you?
And you, you scamps, how dare you steal my Krishna,
　　　　when I told you
That he was ill?
Krishna.　　　　Yes, mother dear;
It's true I'm ill: but never fear;
There's one thing that will cure me.
Yashoda. Oh say, what is that?
Krishna.　　　　　　But will you swear
To let me have it then?
Yashoda.　　　　Why, yes;
Of course I will.
Boys.　　　　If Krishna's ill,
The reason why is easy to guess.
What is his sickness we all know,
And whom he caught it from; and so

R. C. Trevelyan

Do Radha and the Gopis.

Yashoda. How faint he looks. He seems in pain.
Quick, tell me what you want, poor child.

Krishna. A small thing, mother darling.
Just one small pearl from your neck-chain.
You soon shall have it back again,
And new ones too, I promise.

Yashoda. Is *that* all?—There! Take which you will—
Since pining for it has made you ill.
Though I don't quite see why that should be.

Krishna. Now you shall see why, mother.

Boys. What will he do with it? Now shall we know
      whether Krishna
Merely was boasting at random, or meant it in earnest,
When from a pearl he professed he could raise up a
      pearl-tree.
Thoughtfully, see, in the palm of his hand he inspects it.
Doubting he stands in a quandary. O silly Krishna,
Are you a God or a Rishi to work such a wonder?
Nay, but have patience awhile.
See, with a confident smile
How he dibbles the soil with his wand, and with heed
Plants in the hole his miraculous seed!

Yashoda. Krishna! Krishna! What have you done!
Have you buried my pearl? So you meant to make fun
Of your poor old mother before this crew
Of rascally boys? Oh shame on you!

Boys. Mother Yashoda, now dont be a scold.
See, he has covered it up with mould!
With a smile he turns away.
To his lip he sets his flute.
Look! he is going to play.
Does he fancy the pearl will obey,
And striking a root like a seed will shoot

143

Up through the ground to his piping's sound?
Let him pipe for a year and a day,
A pearl is a pearl, I say.
Lalita. [*Aside.*] If Radha had lent him a pearl from
      her ear,
She'd never have seen it again, that's clear.
On a fool she'd have thrown it away.
Sudama. Subala, look, oh look! The soil's lifting!
      there!
Subala. Nonsense! I see nothing. Not a grain's stirred,
      not one.
Sudama. Yes, but it heaves, see! ever so little, just
      there!
Valarama. Wonderful! Yes, it breaks. Pushing its
      way it comes,
A tiny spikelet of grey! The pearl-tree is born, it is born!
Sudama. Oh that Radha were here to see!
Wouldn't she just look foolish now?
Lalita. [*Aside.*] Yes indeed, poor foolish girl!
Subala. What's so wonderful in this tree?
Wait until he can show us a pearl
Hanging upon a pearl-tree bough.
Sudama. Already it's grown seven inches tall.
Valarama. No, ten.
Another Boy.   Why, surely it's over a foot.
Subala. What if it's no real tree atall,
But a false delusion, a cheating charm
Cast over our minds by Krishna's flute?
Sudama. No, for I've touched it. You too try.
It's just as real as you or I.
Another Boy. I've measured it: see, it's as long as my
      arm.
Another. Look at those buds: they're beginning to
      sprout.

R. C. Trevelyan

On every side it's branching out,
Leaf, tendril and shoot.
Subala.   But where's the fruit?
Sudama. Wider and thicker and higher and quicker
It's spreading and curling, expanding, unfurling.
Subala. But I dont see it pearling.
Another Boy. What is that? Do you see? Oh, what
    can it be?
That tiniest grain, as small and bright as the eye
Of a moth or a wren or a blue dragonfly,
Or a droplet of rain!
Oh look, look again! It is growing, it is swelling.
And look, there are others, two, three, four and five!
The whole tree's alive
With dozens and fifties and hundreds past telling
Of pearls, bright pearls.
Every moment they're gleaming both brighter and
    plumper.
See there, what a bumper!
Krishna, our Krishna! There's none like our Krishna.
Oh, what would not Radha and the Gopi girls
Give now to be here?
Krishna. There, mother dear! There's your pearl back
    again.
Yashoda. O Krishna, my joy!
Krishna.   There are some for your ear;
And there's a good handful to make a new chain.
Boys. Come, let us pick them and prick them and thread
    them on twine,
And make of them chains to engarland the necks of our
    kine;
Yes, and our own necks too. Oh, shant we look fine!
Then home to the byres and the milking in triumph
    we'll lead them,

Dancing and frolicking, joking and laughing and singing.
Though the Gopis come weeping and begging and
    clinging,
Not a glance will we give, not a pearl great or small,
Till Radha grow humble, and Krishna forgive.
Lalita. [*Aside.*] Poor Radha, humbled wilt thou be
    indeed;
And for forgiveness sore will be thy need.
Now must I hasten back with my strange news.
Nought truly in the telling shall it lose. [*Exit* LALITA.

SCENE V

The village of Gokula; the same as Scene III.

Lalita.

AH, had you but been there to see!
    Radha.   Yes, then
I might have known the truth.
Lalita.   Why should you doubt me?
Radha. Give me some proof, instead of all these words.
You talk of pearls in myriads; yet not one
Have you brought back to show me.
Lalita.   How could I, Radha?
Did you not bid me keep myself close hidden?
Radha. Well, then?
Lalita.   Why, then I rose and stole away ·
But as I looked back through the leaves I saw
That now from a bush it had become a tree
Tall as the tallest there, its every bough
Glancing and glimmering with a robe of pearls,
One flame of silver fire: and there, high up

R. C. Trevelyan

Among the branches clambering they swarmed
With shouts and laughter, shaking down the pearls,
Others below gathering them as they showered,
Piercing and threading them
Radha.   Piercing indeed!
These pearls of yours must have been strange ones, soft
As grapes or rose-buds to be pierced so easily.
Lalita. Which would you deem the greater miracle,
From a pearl to raise a pearl-tree, or to give power
To pierce with needles his own magic fruit?
Radha. Needles! Whence had these cowherds needles?
       Did
The pearl-tree bear them too?
Lalita.   No, 'twas Yashoda.
She found them needles. And all the while aloof
Stood Krishna, unconcerned, heedless of all
Save his flute's melody; while the enchanted herd
Thronged round him gazing, and forgot to feed.
Radha. Oh, I am out of patience with your mockery.
Lalita. Radha, believe me, I have told you truth,
As an hour hence you'll know, when they come leading
Their cattle home, crowned and festooned with pearls,
Their own necks too like rajahs garlanded.
What then will pride avail you against their ribaldries
And Krishna's vengeful triumph and disdain?
What, save to augment grief's shame? Be wise, and
       seek
That pardon, which he waits for but one word
Freely to give.
Radha.   His pardon! Never, Lalita!
Leave me, leave me. I will not hear you more.
                                        [*Exit* LALITA.

No, I will not believe.—Or if I must,
Yet not for that will I be humble to him.

147

Ah Pride, Pride, thou infidel,
Thou jealous tyrant, why
Art thou so strong, and I,
Thy slave, so weak that I dare not rebel?
Dare not obey my own heart when it calls?
Why is to yield impossible,
Though alone by yielding first
May longed-for happiness be mine?
Thus perishing with love's thirst
By the well's brink I pine.
Already twilight falls.
One thing there is ere it be night
That I must do in pride's despite.
To the jungle must I hasten, and there with my own
    eyes
Learn whether Lalita spoke truth, or was it lies.
Quick, then, while there is light to see!
It was under the sacred peepul tree,
Where sits the old Rishi night and day—
Near Jumna's banks.—I cannot miss the way.   [*Exit.*

SCENE VI

Under the peepul tree, where the RISHI *still sits, as in
Scenes II and III. Enter* RADHA.

Radha.

THE sun sets: night draws round:
  And I am here alone.
How long it seems since last I heard the sound
Of laughter and singing, and so left the path,
Following them in vain! By now they must

R. C. Trevelyan

Have reached the village. Ah!
Yonder is the peepul tree. Is this the place?
But where are they? And he?
And where is   .? Oh my folly   !
If it was here, 'tis vanished. And yet here
They must have been: for the grass is trodden down
By hooves and feet. And there the Rishi sits.
I will approach and speak with him.—Sanyassin,
Tell me, I pray, was Krishna here but now?
Rishi. Who art thou?
Radha.   I am Radha. I seek Krishna,
The son of Nanda. Hast thou not seen him here?
Rishi. Him whom men call Krishna I have seen,
And I have heard his flute.
Radha.   But why has vanished
His pearl-sown tree? Was it not here it grew?
Rishi. Canst thou not see it?
Radha.   No; I see nothing here.
Rishi. The proud in heart see nought. Pride blinds
   their eyes.
Radha. Oh, I am proud no more: yet am I blind.
Rishi. Then thou shalt see perchance, when 'tis his will.
Radha. Alas, weak is my faith: but I repent
My pride and folly now. Thou art wise: tell me,
How may I find my Krishna?
Rishi.   When so he wills.
Radha. Ay me! I have scorned, faithlessly scorned
   him. Now
He scorns and rejects me.
Rishi.   Krishna scorns none
Who seek him with desire.
Radha.   I desire; I seek;
And finding not, must perish. Oh tell me how
Am I to find him?

149

R. C. Trevelyan

Rishi.   That thou alone canst know.
                        [RADHA *turns away.*

Radha. Night falls round me:
Within me is night.
Yonder stars mock me.
In my heart shines
No star, no moon,
No hope of light.
Then death come soon,
Since he
Hath willed it so.
Yet not he, no,
'Twas I who scorned him, I who killed
That light whereby
My life he filled.

Would that again
I might behold my Krishna's face,
But one last glance,
Before I die!
Did not the Rishi say, " Perchance
Thou yet shalt see him, if so he will."
Hope then, hope still
For that last grace,
Though hope be vain.

Oh, what is it there that gleams?
What is it shimmering yonder between the trees?
The pearl-tree! Krishna's pearl-tree! Can it be?
Is it only the moon that rises, silvering Jumna's streams?
There upon either bank
Is it a city I see
In the moonshine glittering bright and white?
Domes and pinnacles height upon height,
Palaces mounting rank beyond rank,

Diamond-glimmering gates and towers,
Sprung from the earth with sudden birth
At some God's whim like magic flowers!
I will go nearer, down to the shores of the river. Oh,
      what may it be?   [*Exit.*

SCENE VII

A group of several Apsaras *stands guarding the gates of a
city, whose walls and pinnacles glitter in the moon-
light.*

Apsaras.

LOVELY beyond all others and delectable
    To the hearts of the Gods are Vrinda's groves:
For by day through their cool solitudes
Frolicking with his playmates
The divine herdsman wanders; and there at nightfall
His flute is heard;
And the melody winding afar down scented paths and
        floating
Over the moon-filled branches, comes to the ears of the
        Gopis,
And their hearts are stirred
By a voice within them pleading:
"Come, come now to the forest. Rise, delay not!
It is I, your Krishna, calls you.
To the forest, to the forest, the moonlight and the dancing!
Follow where the flute is leading!"
Then rising one by one from byre and household,
They steal forth into the night, leaving kine unmilked,
Cradles unrocked, fire and board untended,
With hearts bespelled

R. C. Trevelyan

Following Govinda's flute-notes through the woodways,
To where beside Jumna's banks he stands;
And there on those moon-silvered sands
The dance is knit, and hands meet hands;
And circling round with glancing feet
That flit and fleet, they chant his praises;
And every maiden fondly deems
'Tis none but he
Who is dancing beside her knee to knee;
For to each and all alike it seems
As though such bliss were hers alone,
And no hand by his were held,
No neck embraced, no lips thrilled
By Krishna's, but her own.

Ah brief delusion, as a dream's joy swift-winged!
Vain beguilement! Fleeting union of mortal nature
        with life divine!
The song ceases, the dance fails:
As a moon-glance on the Jumna in splendour revealed,
And anon quenched in cloud-veils, is the God for whom
        they pine.

Then desolate and with grief distraught,
Seeking and calling his name they wander
Hither and thither among the trees.
But of all most bitter is Radha's woe,
Who loving most was most beloved,
And in her heart's proud folly thought
That she alone to the God was dear.
But alas, at pride's lightest breath
Bliss like a bubble vanisheth,
Leaving anger's stubborn pain
And grief that counterfeits disdain.

152

But wisdom now in suffering's school
Hath Radha learnt, poor love-sick fool.
Be it Krishna's will that here
May end her penance and despair!

Enter RADHA.

Radha. Oh, it is strange—yet 'tis no dream.
The place I know, these banks, those trees,
All still the same without a change:
And there below flows Jumna's stream.
But yonder marvellous palaces,
Where yesterday was nought atall,
This city glistening wall above wall,
Towering through the moon's clear light
Into the vastnesses of night—
Can these be real? Or has he
Who from a pearl could raise a tree,
Has he bidden it further by magic power
To expand and unfurl and be changed in an hour
Into a wonderful city of pearl?

Is yonder the gateway? Yes, it is there.
Then will I enter straightway and seek within.
With eyes no longer blind, purged of pride's sin,
Perchance there shall I find by Krishna's grace
His pearl-sown tree, and might that be, behold him
     face to face.

But stay! Who are these
So silent and so stern? Beware!
Hide still 'mid the trees!
I dare not question them.
The splendour of their beauty makes me afraid.
I dare not. They would scorn one such as me.

Yet I must perish if I find not Krishna.
I will approach them.
                              Gracious deities,
Tell me, I pray you, tell me where is Krishna,
Krishna, the son of Nanda and Yashoda?
Suffer me to enter, if he be within.
First Apsara. Who may this be?
Second Apsara.   It is some mad woman.
Radha. I am Radha. I seek Krishna, my beloved.
First Apsara. So, thou art Radha, the foolish cow-girl,
            she
Who deemed in vanity of heart that Krishna
Loved none but her; yet when he begged one pearl,
One small pearl from her neck, refused and mocked
            him.
What, a vile thing such as thou intrude within
These mansions of the Gods! Home to thy milk-pails!
Radha. Drive me not away. Though Krishna scorn me
            still,
And hide his countenance from me, yet perchance,
Could I but find his pearl-tree. . . . Oh, forbid me not
To enter and seek within, if it be there.
Second Apsara. Ah, now we know what brings her here;
            not love
Of Krishna, no, but greed for pearls, gay pearls
To deck her robe and bosom, and so attract
Some cowherd's wanton eyes to her poor charms.
Third Apsara. 'Tis not for such as thou art to behold
The heaven-born pearl-tree. Go then, drown thyself
In thy despair. Yonder is the Jumna. Leap
Within its waves; and they shall carry thee
Down to the sea. There shall thy craving soul
Find pearls in plenty to content its greed.
Radha. Ah, mock me; but have pity, and let me pass.

Fourth Apsara. Whither? There is no pearl-tree any
       more.
By its own weight of fruitage overladen
Its stem cracked and it fell; and with the fruits
Did Krishna build these palaces and towers,
A paradise of pearl for their delight
Whom most he loves. And therefore stand we here
To guard these gates from covetous coquettes.
Radha. Yet, I beseech you, open, and from the threshold
Let me but look within.
Third Apsara.   Away, shrill gnat!
Fifth Apsara. Sisters, let us be pitiful so far.
If she be shown that where this pearl-tree stood
There is none now, then will she be content
To depart humbly as beseems a mortal.
Radha. Yes, I will be content. But open quickly.
      [*The* Apsaras *open the gates of the city. A
          street with a vista of shining buildings is
          revealed.*
Fifth Apsara. Behold! What seest thou?
Radha.   Nothing but light I see.
The light of pearls is everywhere.—The pearl-tree!
It must come from the pearl-tree. Where, where is it?
Let me pass! I must find it, or die here.
Oh, do not stay me.
First Apsara.   Further to relent
Were but a cruel kindness to thee, Radha.
For know that like a fevered child's dreamland,
Grown monstrous with enormity's despair,
So infinite are those concentric mazes
Which thou must travel inward, street on street,
Gate beyond gate, city within city,
Till old and feeble, after countless years,
It may be thou shalt reach Vaikuntha's paradise,

R. C. Trevelyan

Krishna's divine abode. There with dimmed eyes
Thou mayst behold a pearl-tree; or perchance
Thou mayst not. Wilt thou venture, thus forewarned?
Radha. Yes, I must venture: I must follow still
Where the light leads. See, palace beyond palace,
Another and another without end,
Brighter and vaster still they tower and dazzle;
Still would they lead me onward, like a moth
Within a feasting chamber, to my doom.
First Apsara. Then pass within. Foolhardy soul, fare-
    well!

        [RADHA *steps through the gateway. At the
        same moment the city vanishes. She turns
        round in amazement, to find that the wall
        and the* APSARAS *have vanished also.*

Radha. Ah! Darkness!
The lights are vanished.
There is no city.

      [*She turns back again: the pearl-tree stands
          before her.*

Oh wonder! It is there!
Oh thou, my life's new light!
Have I now found thee? Do I touch thee now?
Vanish not as those mocking phantoms did.
Ah cruelly, yet blessedly, they mocked me:
For they through scorn have led me to this joy.
See how the ground glimmers with fallen pearls!
Yet still the boughs with clustering thousands droop,
Laden to overflowing, as my heart with bliss.

But why do I feel this rapture?
What else are they but only pearls and moonlight?
Why did I vex my soul for moonlit pearls?
Had I not pearls enough at home? Alas,

R. C. Trevelyan

How could I prove so miserly of my store,
When 'twas my love that begged?—Ah cruel Krishna!
Is this thy vengeance? Hast thou lured me hither
To mock me with the emblem of my shame?
Not for thy pearl-tree's splendour, but for the light
Of thine eyes was I pining. Spurned by thee,
Denied thy pardon, here must death find me.
Below me is the ripple of the Jumna.
Were it not best? . . . Why, when the light is quenched,
Not cast the lamp from me?

O Krishna! Krishna!
Lord of my soul! Lord of the universe!
I am but a poor foolish woman, frail,
Ignorant, vile as dust. Have pity on me.
Oh pardon me, my Lord: forsake me not,
Weak, sinful, shameful, worthless though I be.
I cannot live without thee. I die here.

> [*She kneels, hiding her face in her hands. The
> pearl-tree fades, and* KRISHNA *is seen
> standing in its place. He steps to* RADHA'S
> *side and touches her arm.*

Krishna. Radhika, my soul's joy, my life's delight!
Where hast thou been all this long weary while?

> [RADHA *prostrates herself and clasps his feet.*
> KRISHNA *raises her up and embraces her.*

Krishna. Come, Radhika, think not upon things past.
Are they not vanished now like evil dreams?
Young is the night yet; and in these lone woods
We two are here alone.

Nay, keep thy pearls.
I need none; for Love's pearl once more is mine.

> [*He restores to her neck the necklace of pearls,
> which she has put into his hands.*

CHISWICK PRESS: CHARLES WHITTINGHAM AND CO.
TOOKS COURT, CHANCERY LANE, LONDON.

Made in the USA
Coppell, TX
09 May 2021

55118969R00095